THE ARCHITECTURE OF
SUPERCOMPUTERS

TITAN, A CASE STUDY

THE ARCHITECTURE OF SUPERCOMPUTERS

TITAN, A CASE STUDY

DANIEL P. SIEWIOREK

Department of Computer Science
Carnegie-Mellon University
Pittsburgh, Pennsylvania

PHILIP JOHN KOOPMAN, JR.

Department of Electrical and Computer Engineering
Carnegie-Mellon University
Pittsburgh, Pennsylvania

ACADEMIC PRESS, INC.
Harcourt Brace Jovanovich, Publishers
Boston   San Diego   New York
London   Sydney   Tokyo   Toronto

This book is printed on acid-free paper.

ACADEMIC PRESS, INC.
1250 Sixth Avenue, San Diego, CA 92101

United Kingdom Edition published by
ACADEMIC PRESS LIMITED
24–28 Oval Road, London NW1 7DX

Library of Congress Cataloging-in-Publication Data

Siewiorek, Daniel P.
    The architecture of supercomputers : Titan, a case study / Daniel
P. Siewiorek, Philip John Koopman, Jr.
        p.   cm.
    Includes bibliographical references (p.   ) and index.
    ISBN 0-12-643060-8 (alk. paper)
    1. Supercomputers.   2. Computer architecture.   I. Koopman, Phil,
1960–   . II. Title.
QA76.5.S536   1991
004.1'1—dc20   90-1276
                                                                      CIP

Printed in the United States of America
91 92 93 94   9 8 7 6 5 4 3 2 1

CONTENTS

To Benjamin, Gail, and Nora

FOREWORD

In December 1985, when the founders were deciding to form Ardent Computer Corporation, I argued that we simply use multiple, MIPS Computer System Inc.'s microprocessors in a multiprocessor configuration in order to get a high performance computer for the technical marketplace. Such a computer would also be useful for the traditional timesharing user who needed lots of mips.

As the company formed in January 1986 and moved forward, the design increased in complexity with the addition of the vector processing unit, turning it into a product Ardent called the graphics supercomputer.[1] The likelihood greatly increased that a product could be designed within the 18 months from the company's formation at a sales price of $50,000 as described in the business plan. It turned out that Titan took 30 months to design (a schedule fantasy factor of about 1.7) and the selling price was $80,000 (a factor of 1.6 over the plan). The first Titan provided substantially more power as a supercomputer with 4 vector processors than a sim-

---

[1] A Supercomputer has evolved to mean the fastest technical computer that can be built at a given time and using the Cray-style, multiple, vector processor architecture. Mini-supercomputers were introduced to mean the fastest computer for about $1 million. A graphics supercomputer was supposed to be a personal supercomputer costing around $50,000.

I place the following constraint on anything called a supercomputer—such a computer must be able to deliver the same computation to a user that the user would obtain on a "true" shared, supercomputer.

ple, multiprocessor would have delivered. In fact, to obtain the same peak power for scientific users would require a factor of 4 more, or 16 scalar processors. The second version of Titan won the 1990 prize for being the most cost-effective computer as measured by the University of Illinois Perfect Club Benchmarks. I'm proud to be associated with the design team and their product. They're probably the best team of this size I've ever worked with.[2]

When I came back to head R&D at Ardent Computer Company in the fall of 1987 to help finish the product design, I contacted Professor Siewiorek about writing a book on the design of Titan, the first graphics supercomputer. In January 1986, after helping Ardent form, I went off to start up the National Science Foundation's Computer and Information Science and Engineering Directorate as its first assistant director. This directorate was also responsible for NSF's five, national supercomputer centers, and I spent two years at NSF also being concerned with providing computing and networking for the research community. This is not unlike the past 25 years I spent at Digital Equipment Corporation, where I was responsible for DEC computers, most of which were designed for the technical marketplace.

If one characterizes computers as MISC (minimal instruction set computer, such as the first computers and early minicomputers), RISC (reduced instruction set), or CISC (complex or complete), the modern supercomputer should be characterized as an UCISC (ultra-complex, since it has operations on vector data-types). A supercomputer implementation is even more complex than the architecture would imply because of the need to execute multiple instructions at once, each of which are operating on multiple independent data elements. When something goes wrong while a program is executing (say a page fault), several hundred data items may be somewhere in transit associated with the context of a processor. It's easy to see why Seymour Cray doesn't provide paging or memory management hardware beyond a single relocation register. Thus, another reason to study Titan is the complexity necessary for vector processing, caching, and paging. Only DEC's VAX 9000 is more complex in its architecture (a CISC with a vector instruction set), its implementation (because it has to go fast to compete with the RISC microprocessors), and its packaging technology. Yet the 9000 provides no graphics and not a great deal more computation capability, even though it costs almost an order of magnitude more to buy and probably a factor of 50 times more to design.

---

[2] The VAX team, though larger, was probably the most talented team. However, VAX and the first implementation, the VAX 11/780, was considerably simpler and highly evolutionary based on the PDP-11.

The motivation for the book was that I was especially proud of the design team and what they had accomplished. In only two and a half years since the beginning of the company, the team designed and shipped a state of the art multiple vector, processor computer (i.e., a supercomputer) that, in addition, had the ability to transform and display almost 100,000 3D polygons per second. Thus, a team of under 50 had designed and built a product that a large company would take at least 4 years and almost 10 times the staff to accomplish. Titan included not only Glen Miranker's architecture, Richard Lowenthal and Jon Rubenstein's hardware, with a dozen custom chips, Tom Diede's graphics subsystem, but Randy Allen's parallelizing, vectorizing compiler, Way Ting's enhancements to UNIX to support multithread operation so that a loop could be executed on multiple processors, Mike Kaplan's great graphics environment, Doré, that enabled a user to exploit the graphics hardware, and Bill Worley's insight and code on numerous parts of the design where speed was essential. I also felt that a book might also help encourage the sale and use of Titan.

In addition to self-serving motivations, I felt strongly that a book on a really good product design is the best way to help others understand the design process and a particular design.[3] I like to read such books (e.g., Bucholz's book on the IBM Stretch, and Thornton's book on the CDC 6600) and write papers, and to read books about design too (Bell and Newell, *Computer Structures: Readings and Examples,* 1971; Siewiorek, Bell, and Newell, *Computer Structures: Principles and Examples,* 1982; and Bell, Mudge, and McNamara, *Computer Engineering: A DEC View of Hardware Design*). There are no books on supercomputer design, and I feel this one is essential for future designers. All modern supercomputers of Convex, Cray, Fujitsu, Hitachi, IBM (with its vector attachment to the 370 architecture), and NEC are organized according to the principles given in this book.

Finally, this book has turned out to be a really good book about architecture generally, simply because Titan uses nearly all the techniques that one would expect in a modern, high speed computer. I hope engineers

---

[3] The reader might look at my own critical view of Titan, which is given in a video lecture on Titan: 11 Rules for Supercomputer Design and available through University Video Communication, Box 2666, Stanford, Ca. 94309. Ardent and Titan are also described in the book, High Technology Ventures, Addison-Wesley, Reading Massachusetts (Bell and McNamara, 1991) about start-up companies. This view includes the various marketing constraints and a discussion of why the first design, P2 lacked the critical scalar performance that made it vulnerable in the market place until the second processor, P3 was introduced. In fact, given the complexity of a supercomputer, it is essential to do a second one following the first, to fix all the flaws inherent in doing a complex design "right" the first time. All "first" supercomputers by an organization have been flawed in some fashion and have required redesign.

designing microprocessors at the various semicomputer companies read and learn from it.

Chapter 1 provides an overview of the Titan architecture, together with the motivation, organization and processes that created it. The design and manufacturing processes are particularly critical because of Titan's size and complexity. The overall schedule of the project is given, inlcuding the design of the state-of-the-art compiler for Fortran to handle multiple, vector processors by parallelization and vectorization.

Chapter 2 presents a survey of all the techniques to speed up computation, including the different types of processors and how they are sped up (e.g., pipelined instruction execution as in RISC), cache memories to reduce memory latency, multiprocessing, memory interleaving, and specialization for graphics (Titan colors pixels at over 50 million per second). Titan uses all known techniques except the wide instruction word, whereby multiple instructions are executed at a single clock cycle by one processor. Instead, multiple independent processors are used for speed-up.

Performance is discussed in Chapter 3. The issue of particular benchmarks such as the Livermore Fortran Kernel Loops and measures such as the harmonic mean are described. The first model, P2, introduced in the spring of 1988, provided a peak of 16 million floating point operations per second (megaflops) and a harmonic mean of about 2 megaflops on the Livermore Loops per processor. The second processor, P3, introduced in the fall of 1989, provided twice the peak power and a harmonic mean of over 5 megaflops. It achieves nearly 100 megaflops for the 1000×1000 Linpack benchmark. The former measure implies the ability to carry out almost ¼ of the work of a Cray YMP processor.

Chapter 4 is brief, but posits a model of a concurrency hierarchy extending from the register set to the entire operating system.

Chapter 5 describes the architecture of Titan graphics supercomputer and its implementation. Given the nature of modern, Cray-style design vector, supercomputers require the ability to load or store a vector register set of 32–64, 64-bit words at a rapid rate. The single most important design issue is the availability of memory bandwidth and the coupling (a switch) of the processors to the memory subsystem. Cray estimates that over half the cost of their supercomputers is in the memory and switch. Titan uses a bus to communicate between its multiple processors and multiple memory. Details of the protocol are given in Appendix A. As such, it is easy to build a multiprocessor, which I defined in 1985 as a "multi" that maintains coherence among all of the processor's cache memories. Designers at the various semicomputer companies designing cost-effective multiprocessors should simply read and copy Titan's bus protocols. Users should demand a well-designed bus because it is at the heart of performance. Titan uses the MIPS microprocessor for integer and floating point scalar operations (P3) to control a vector processing unit. The architecture of the MIPS scalar processor, Ardent's vector processing element (which the scalar processor controls), and the graphics processor architectures and implementations are given.

Chapter 6 analyzes the performance of Titan in terms of the various information flow data rates.

Chapter 7 looks at the actual performance on benchmark kernels and how the architecture and implementation affect performance. The authors also quote and discuss my Eleven Rules for Supercomputer Design.

I strongly recommend this book by Siewiorek and Koopman as a text or supplementary text in architecture and computer design courses. I also believe it is useful and essential for architects and engineers designing new processors and systems. The authors have done an excellent job of capturing the design issues inherent in a high performance, multiple, vector-processor computer, including the special issues of graphics processing.

Gordon Bell

PREFACE

The stored program digital computer has been in existence fewer than 50 years. Yet in that half century there have been at least six generations, several thousand models, and tens of millions of computers fabricated. Some computers were one of a kind, while others emerged to dominate an industry. As the cost of technology decreased, computers emerged that defined new classes of applications.

As in human history, many of the events in computer design have been recorded in logic schematics and technical manuals that are not only hard to obtain but difficult to decipher. On rare occasions a book will be written that not only provides details for the various interlocking pieces but also provides insights as to why the pieces are shaped the way they are. The goal of this book is to describe the architecture of the first member of an entirely new computing class—the graphic supercomputing workstation. The motivation for defining a new class of computer architectures as well as the form of the architecture that responds to the specifications for this new class are described.

This book has two audiences: technical professionals and students. For technical professionals, a study of the Titan architecture yields insights into an historically significant machine. For students, the relatively small size of Titan makes it possible to examine its architectural principles in isolation as well as to gain an understanding of the interdependencies of the various design decisions. Even though the Titan architecture is relatively compact, it employs many of the techniques used by high-performance supercomputers. Rather than simply describing the architecture, the book employs a taxonomy as a means for organizing the discussion. Since performance is of paramount importance, a separate taxonomy and discussion on performance metrics is provided.

The material illuminates in a top-down manner various subsystems and their interactions in successively greater detail. By abstracting out unnecessary detail, the reader can focus on the issues central to the discussion. The multiple passes also provide a moderate amount of repetition so that by the end of the book the reader firmly grasps the architecture as a whole rather than a disjoint pile of subsystems.

Chapters Two and Three provide an evolutionary discussion of architectural and performance concepts. These chapters have been provided so that the book is self-contained. The experienced reader may skip these chapters without loss of continuity. Likewise, Section 2 in Chapter One provides a quick, high-level summary of the major features of the Titan architecture. Since many of these terms may be unfamiliar to the student reader, this section can be postponed until Chapters Two and Three have been studied in detail.

Each of the chapters in this book has a well-defined goal. Chapter One motivates the need for a new class of computers. It describes the Titan architecture at a high level as an example of one possible architectural concept that satisfies the specifications for this new computer class. The chapter concludes with a brief history of the company and the development process that culminated in the first customer shipment of the Titan computer. Chapter Two provides a taxonomy of techniques in the design of high-performance computers. Each technique is motivated and examples of its use in Titan are described. These techniques form the basic building blocks for any high-performance computer design. Chapter Three introduces the concept of performance measurement and balance in a computer architecture. A taxonomy of architectural metrics for measuring performance is provided. The chapter focuses on the concept of "balance" in an architecture as well as between major subsystems.

A typical application for a graphic supercomputer is described in Chapter Four. Mapping of various phases of the computation onto the high-level model of Titan sets the stage for understanding design trade-offs described in the rest of the book. Chapter Five describes the implementation details for the various subsystems in the Titan architecture. Using these details, Chapter Six conducts an architectural analysis that demonstrates the interrelationships between the performance provided by each subsystem as well as the balance of the entire Titan architecture. Finally, Chapter Seven demonstrates the effectiveness of the theory employed in the development of the architecture. Several benchmarks demonstrate that the Titan architecture comes arbitrarily close to realizing its theoretically predicted maximum performance. This chapter culminates with a set of 11 rules for designing supercomputers that were compiled by Gordon Bell during the design of the Titan architecture.

Several pedagogical mechanisms are used to support the reader. In addition to the top-down refinement approach to describe the architecture, several examples are spread throughout the text to reinforce the architectural discussions. Appendix A provides a more detailed description of the bus system, which forms the heart of the Titan architecture. Appendix B contains a summary of the major features of the Titan architecture that may serve as a quick reference for the design decisions discussed in detail throughout the book. Appendix C contains a glossary with concise definitions of the major terms and concepts.

ACKNOWLEDGMENTS

Numerous people at Stardent made their material and time generously available so that this book could be written. In particular, we would like to thank Gordon Bell, Glen Miranker, Jon Rubenstein, John Sanguinetti, Agha Ahsan, Bill Worley, Cleve Moler, Jose Aguirre, Peter Pappanastos, and David Dobras. Paul Ausick at Stardent, Kim Faught at Carnegie Mellon University, and Alice Peters at Academic Press provided able assistance in production of the manuscript. We would like particularly to acknowledge the hard work of Mark Holland and Laura Forsyth without whom this manuscript could not have been completed.

Daniel P. Siewiorek
Philip J. Koopman, Jr.

TITAN
ARCHITECTURE
OVERVIEW

This chapter is a brief introduction to the first-generation Titan architecture, including the design priorities and a simplified overview of the architecture. The chapter also discusses the history of the design and construction of Titan, a topic which is usually overlooked in the discussion of a computer architecture.

For those who are familiar with the terminology used to describe vector multiprocessor computer architectures (i.e., supercomputers), this chapter will provide a concise high-level description. For those not already familiar with this notation, it will serve as a general orientation and provide a list of new concepts that will be fully described in later chapters. The purpose of providing this initial overview is to present a concrete architecture as a basis for general discussions on design issues in later chapters. But first, let's explore the premises upon which the architecture was based—premises that led to the definition of a new class of computers. Closely coupled to the architectural vision is the strategic plan to bring an implementation to market in a timely manner.

1.1 VISUALIZATION OF SCIENTIFIC COMPUTATIONS

In the fall of 1985, there was a confluence of several technologies that made the Titan project possible. Computational power as represented by

Cray-class computers had decreased in cost from the multimillion dollar range to the several hundred thousand dollar range with the introduction of the so-called super minicomputer. Typically designed from custom gate array chips, these uniprocessors incorporated many of the features of supercomputers such as vector hardware and vectorizing compilers. The advent of high-performance RISC microprocessors and stock commercial floating point chips provided the opportunity for incorporating system architectural principles, which formerly could only be applied in super-computer-class machines, into smaller systems with a substantial cost reduction.

A second trend was the popularity of the engineering workstation—a uniprocessor system dedicated to a single user. The cost of computers had decreased so dramatically that a complete workstation with processor, memory, secondary storage, network interconnection, and graphics display cost about as much as a first generation video display. The economics were now at a point where it made sense to provide each engineering or scientific professional with a dedicated computer. A substantial proportion of the computer's resources was devoted to providing an effective coupling between the human and the machine. Scientific visualization was coming to computing. Indeed, workstations were tied to supercomputers through local area networks so that computational results that were previously large printouts of floating point numbers could be translated into graphical images. However, the results produced by a computation that took only minutes to run on a supercomputer often took hours to transmit over a relatively low bandwidth local-area network to an engineering workstation, where it was transformed into a graphical image; furthermore, these images were restricted to black and white.

A third technology was high-performance color graphics. The algorithms required to turn a list of points and vectors into a realistic, shaded color image had been refined and implemented in a number of high-end graphics engines. Wire-frame surfaces could be clipped to remove the surfaces not visible from the chosen viewing perspective; the remaining surfaces could be shaded as a function of the selected characteristics of lighting sources. Animation could be achieved by continually performing these computations and displaying them as screen images.

By merging these technologies, the concept of visualized computation was conceived. The advances in semiconductor technology could be used to design a high-performance scientific workstation whose numerical processing power was previously only available in supercomputer class machines. This processing power could not only be used to perform the scientific computations, but also to perform the computations required to display the data. By dedicating a workstation to a single scientist or engineer, interactive experiments or designs could be conducted wherein the user modified the input data and almost immediately visualized the effect of the change. It would no longer be necessary to wait several hours to visualize the results of a parameter change in a computational model.

For Titan to succeed in the marketplace, the computational power had to be equal to that available from a true supercomputer to one of a number of shared users for a lower cost/performance ratio (in other words, job execution measured by wall clock time for a single-user Titan and a time-shared Cray had to be equivalent with a lower pro-rated computational cost for the Titan). The graphics had to be of extremely high quality for near photorealistic graphics. The system also had to be capable of interactive simulations, not just batch-mode computations. The combination of high-performance computation and high-quality graphics had to be provided on a platform that was immediately accessible to the user in real time—in other words, it had to appear to be a workstation-type environment with supercomputer performance in order to be useful for interactive problem solving. Thus, the design goal for Titan became the creation of a new class of computers, the "graphics minisupers."

The goal of the Titan architecture is therefore to provide a single-user supercomputer with the ability to visualize the results of complex computations. To achieve this goal, Titan needs to provide high performance by using an attached vector processor at reasonably low cost. Typical applications for single-user visualization supercomputers are primarily scientific and engineering programs. These programs typically require a large amount of floating-point arithmetic on single variables as well as vectors and matrices[1] which have hitherto been the domain of very large supercomputers such as those made by Cray Research, Inc.

In addition to fast floating point computations, a single-user supercomputer should also provide high quality interactive graphics. These graphics enable a user to interpret the tremendous amount of data that may be produced by a computation. Typical applications include: computational fluid dynamics, finite element analysis, molecular dynamics, and three-dimensional solid modeling. Specifications for the Titan architecture were derived from attributes of the scientific visualization domain.

Because Titan is often used as a single-user supercomputer, *absolute speed to solve a single problem is more important than overall throughput*. The criterion for success as a personal supercomputer is not that the system be as fast as a mainframe supercomputer, but rather that jobs be completed in less wall clock time (i.e., time as measured by the clock on the user's

---

[1] A vector is a linear collection of variables that can be manipulated as a group. Similarly, matrices are a two-dimensional collection of variables.

office wall, not elapsed CPU time) than jobs submitted to the user's main-frame supercomputer. Let us suppose that the Titan can complete some computation in one hour, and the average wait in a job queue on the local Cray mainframe is two hours. Then the Titan is faster than the Cray, as perceived by the user, no matter how little time the Cray takes to perform the actual computation.

Titan also supports multiuser operation. In this mode of operation, the Titan provides high-performance computational facilities at a small frac-tion of the cost of a supercomputer; however, design tradeoffs have been made to reduce cost in favor of single-user computing speed rather than multiuser throughput.

To reach a compromise between the demands of high performance and low cost, Titan provides only those specialized hardware resources that are absolutely necessary for high performance, then reuses these resources in a variety of modes. For example, the vectorized floating-point unit is used not only for scientific and engineering floating-point computations, but also for three-dimensional clipping and transformations for the graphics display programs.

To reduce development time and costs (which are reflected in the time-to-market and end-product cost), Titan uses off-the-shelf components where possible. Major system components that were purchased for use in the system include the integer processor unit, the floating-point arithmetic chips, and the graphics rendering chips. Also, exotic technologies were avoided wherever possible to reduce the engineering design costs and potential problems (for example, ECL technology is only used in time-crit-ical areas of the bus interface, whereas TTL and CMOS are used elsewhere in the design).

The result of these tradeoffs is a machine suitable for use both as a sin-gle-user supercomputer as well as a high-speed general-purpose computer for multiple users (i.e., a minisuper). As we shall see, the concept of bal-ancing resources in terms of capacities is crucial to the cost effectiveness and speed of Titan.

1.2   SYSTEM OVERVIEW

A high-level block diagram of Titan is shown in Figure 1.1. The Titan archi-tecture consists of a shared system bus, a memory subsystem, between one and four processors (each with separate integer and vector floating-point execution hardware), a graphics display subsystem, and an I/O subsystem. Figure 1.2 depicts a Titan system in greater detail.

The following sections are intended to give a brief introduction to the

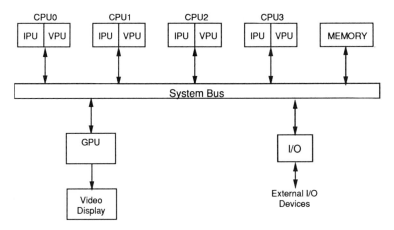

FIGURE 1.1. High-level block diagram of Titan.

Titan architecture. If some terms are unfamiliar, do not worry. All the material will be explained in much greater detail in subsequent chapters.[2]

1.2.1 SYSTEM BUS

Since Titan is a high-performance multiprocessor, the heart of the system is its bus. This bus must meet heavy data-traffic demands of the integer and floating-point processors, the graphics processor, and the I/O subsystem simultaneously. Multiprocessors are commonly limited by available bus bandwidth, so providing the bus with the most bandwidth possible was an important design priority.

Titan uses a global synchronous system bus for all its data movement. The bus has two 64-bit data paths to accomplish transfers: the S-BUS and the R-BUS. The S-BUS (store bus) is a read/write bus that is used for general-purpose access to memory and vector store operations. The R-BUS (read bus) is a second bus which, by hardware convention, is used only for reading from memory by vector processors.

The bus transaction frequency and the main clock frequency of Titan is 16 MHz (62.5 ns per cycle). All bus transactions, as well as the integer processing unit (IPU) and vector processing unit (VPU), are synchronized to a global system clock. Thus data can be transferred at the rate of $2 \times 16 \times 8 = 256$ MBytes/sec using both the R and S buses.

---

[2] The remainder of Section 1.2 may be skipped on a first reading by those unfamiliar with the terminology. This material can be read after Chapter 2.

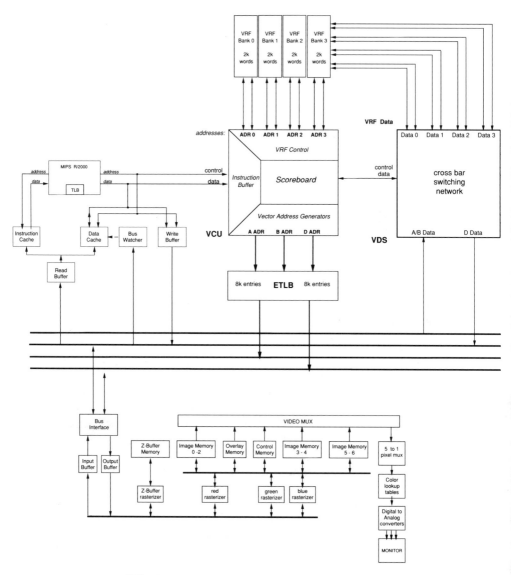

FIGURE 1.2.   An overview of the Titan architecture.

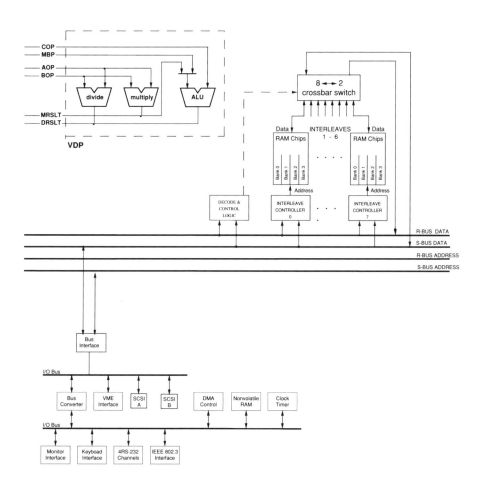

1.2.2   MEMORY

Closely coupled to the bus is the memory subsystem. Most communication traffic on the system bus is between memory and the various processors. In addition to rapidly supplying great quantities of data, the memory must be large enough to hold the huge data sets often encountered in scientific programs.

The Titan system uses a memory hierarchy including virtual memory, physical memory, cache memory, and register files. Physical memory is organized with interleaves to increase available bandwidth. Each memory card in the system is dual-ported, allowing both the R-BUS and the S-BUS to access the same memory cards on every bus cycle.

1.2.3   CPU

Titan can be configured with between one and four central processors. Each processor contains an Integer Processing Unit (IPU) and a Vector Processing Unit (VPU).

1.2.3.1   INSTRUCTION FETCH AND INTEGER PROCESSING UNIT (IPU)

The IPU is built around the MIPS R2000 reduced instruction set computer (RISC). The IPU is used for integer scalar processing and for issuing instructions to the VPU. The IPU (Figure 1.2) is supported by separate instruction- and data-cache memory and a write buffer.

1.2.3.2   VECTOR PROCESSING UNIT (VPU)

Each VPU (Figure 1.2) consists of a Vector Control Unit (VCU), a Vector Data Switch (VDS), a Vector Data Path (VDP), and a Vector Register File (VRF). In the first version of Titan, both scalar and vector floating-point operations are carried out in the VPU.

The VCU controls the operation of the other parts of the VPU. It contains the address generators for addressing vectors in both memory and the VRF as well as a scoreboard for allowing out-of-order execution of instruction through *chaining* and *hazard detection*.

The VDS routes data between sections of the VPU. It allows routing of data between memory, the VRF, and the VDP.

The VDP provides the actual computation power of the VPU. It can operate on both floating-point and fixed-point data and contains special-purpose hardware for a pipelined ALU, a pipelined multiplier, and a divider.

The VRF acts as high-speed storage for the VPU. By using a generalization of the typical supercomputer vector-register concept, the VRF may be organized under software control for any combination of scalar and vector quantities.

1.2.4 GRAPHICS PROCESSING UNIT (GPU)

The graphics processing unit (GPU) is an auxiliary processor that contains memory for a high-resolution color graphics display as well as special hardware to support fast graphics operations. With the graphics expansion card installed, the graphics memory can hold two full-color (8 bits each of red, green, and blue) high-resolution images in its frame buffers. The GPU also has a 16-bit Z-buffer for depth annotation. Four hardware pixel processors (one each for red, green, blue, and Z-buffer) provide fast hardware support for line and shaded triangle drawing. The output of the GPU goes to a video display.

1.2.5 I/O PROCESSING

The I/O subsystem provides access to external I/O devices. It provides an interface to disk drives for file storage and virtual memory via two SCSI (Small Computer–System Interface) buses. Access is also provided to a VME bus, as well as an on-board "microbus," which connects Ethernet, UARTs, the printer, the keyboard, and the mouse to the S-BUS.

1.3 GENERAL OPERATION PRINCIPLES

Within Titan, the IPUs provide most control functions. They not only execute the integer code for the system (which includes conditional branches, looping structures, and the like), but also control other resources. For example, the IPU feeds instructions to the VPU to accomplish vector operations. The IPU also builds graphics command lists in memory that are executed by the GPU.

The VPU is used for all floating-point operations. The VPU can process both scalar and vector quantities; it also provides hazard and chaining detection and resolution completely in hardware. The VPU is used by programs both for floating-point numeric computations and for graphics coordinate transformations.

The GPU executes commands from data structures (display lists) placed into memory by the IPU. The GPU has direct hardware support for line drawing, for filled, shaded triangle drawing, and for block memory transfers.

The IPU and VPU of each installed CPU, the GPU, and I/O events may

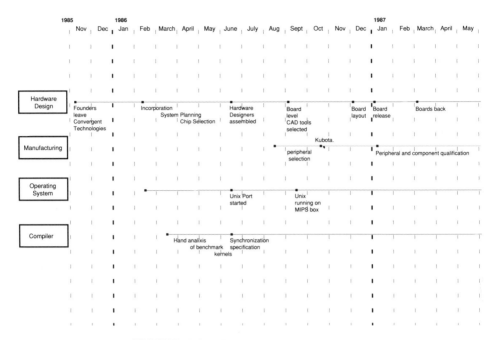

FIGURE 1.3.   Timeline of the Titan project.

all operate simultaneously within the system to achieve parallel program execution.

1.4   FROM CONCEPT TO REALIZATION

1.4.1   BACKGROUND

Figure 1.3 gives an overview of the major events in the conception, design, and implementation of the Titan graphics supercomputer. In the fall of 1985 the founders of Stardent Computer left their jobs at Convergent Technologies.[3] Many scientists in universities and government were contacted to assess their interest in a graphics supercomputing workstation. Ideas were collected, and the company was incorporated in the spring of 1986.

---

[3] The company's name was originally Dana Computer. Because of a naming conflict with another company, this was changed to Ardent in 1988. Then, as a result of a merger with Stellar Computer, the name was changed to Stardent in 1989. We shall use the name Stardent throughout the book for the sake of consistency but in all cases will refer to the portion of the current Stardent company that traces its roots back to Ardent and Dana Computer.

| | June | July | Aug | Sept | Oct | Nov | Dec | **1988** Jan | Feb | March | April | May | June | July | Aug | Sept | Oct | Nov | Dec | **1989** Jan | Feb |

Timeline milestones:

- 5 P0 machines
- 5 P1 machines
- Strife Testing
- P1 Beta
- ten P1 machines from Kubota
- Outside Beta
- FCS
- P2
- Multiuser Login prompt-self hosting
- Vector unit support
- Full kernel stable OS
- Rebuild Compiler
- Compiler Tuning

Once the major features of the system had been identified, the task at hand was the hiring of key individuals with expertise in the vast array of disciplines required to bring the system to fruition. Experts in hardware design, operating systems, vectorizing/parallelizing compilers, graphics, and computational algorithms were identified and brought on board to provide further refinement to the systems plans. By April of 1986, more than 20 individuals had been gathered to work on the project.

The first half of 1986 was an interactive give-and-take between system architects, the operating system designers, and the compiler designers. As the machine evolved, it was clear that there was a cost/performance potential for an exciting new class of computing; however, the machine could not succeed without an operating system and an optimizing compiler designed to harness that potential. The software task was even more difficult because there were no pre-existing systems with the attributes of the supercomputing graphics workstation. While software planning, design, and implementation had to proceed in parallel with hardware design, it would be over a year before hardware representing the target system would be available for operating system and compiler development.

By June of 1986, the hardware and software teams had been established.

The following subsections will illustrate how these design teams interacted over the following two years to converge on a first customer shipment (FCS) in July of 1988.

1.4.2   HARDWARE DESIGN

1.4.2.1   BEGINNINGS

Figure 1.4 shows a timeline of the hardware design process for Titan. System conceptual planning occurred during the spring of 1986. This was

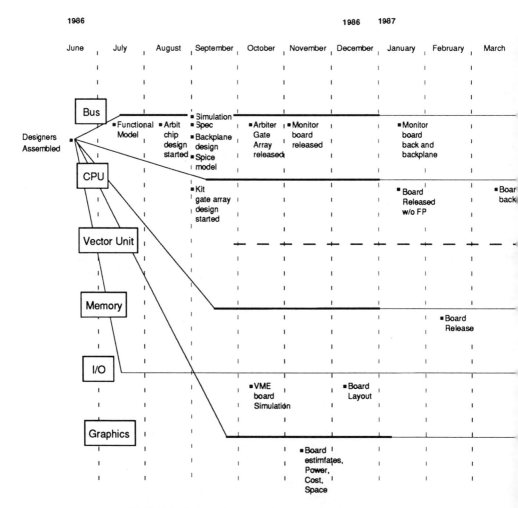

FIGURE 1.4.   Timeline of the hardware design process.

followed by an intense search to identify semiconductor chips which would be used for key portions of the system such as the integer processor, floating-point arithmetic chips, and graphics rasterizers. By May of 1986, an estimate for board size, power consumption, and cost were established. The original target was for a $50,000 system achieving three MFLOPS (million floating operations per second).

The design process was divided into four major phases: schematic capture, simulation, timing verification, and translations to formats for physical layout. Valid Logic's schematic capture software was used to describe

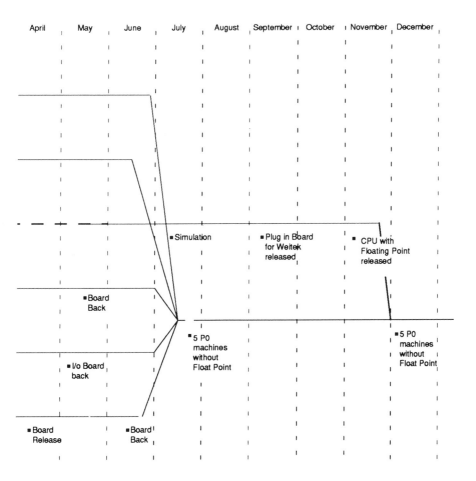

the design in a hierarchical fashion. The modules in the schematic hierarchy were carefully selected to be a superset of both the physical hierarchy and the behavioral module hierarchy used in simulation and timing verification. Small portions of the design were simulated using the Valid gate-level logic simulator. Multi-level simulation was used to verify the system design. Components that were not involved in the operation under scrutiny were represented at the highest levels of abstraction. Components that take part in the operation but whose detailed behavior is not the subject of study are represented at an intermediate level of abstraction. The register transfer and gate levels of abstraction represented the most detail. Verilog-XL provided mixed-level behavioral, register transfer, and gate-level simulation. A translator from Valid netlists produced Verilog source statements. For example, a simulation model to test the operation of a floating-point vector pipeline would consist of the following modules:

- Functional Level. Memory, adder/multiplier/divider, cache, and integer-processing unit.
- Register Transfer Level. Crossbar and vector data paths.
- Gate Level. Scoreboard, load/store pipe, operational pipe, and vector register file.

Timing verification was performed by ValidTime. Delays were estimated and refined as physical layout information became available.

Design verification consisted of executing tests on the simulation model. The first approach executed diagnostic programs; however, diagnostic programs spend most of their time checking results of the operation of interest and hence consume a great deal of simulation time. The second approach replaced the integer processor by a behavioral model of its interface. To the rest of the system, the integer processor merely reads or writes cache or memory locations. The behavioral model of the processor read commands from a test file and simulated the loads and stores to appropriate addresses. The behavioral model also had the ability to check the internal state in response to commands in the test file. For example, the results of a floating-point operation could be checked simply by examining the contents of the result register rather than simulating the execution of a compare instruction. Small pieces of logic were exhaustively tested while larger pieces of logic with tens of bits of internal state were tested randomly.

It is clear that modeling and simulation played an important part in the overall design process. Verilog (Gateway, 1987) was selected as the primary simulation tool early in the design cycle. Verilog was chosen because it provided enough descriptive capability to model components at functional, register transfer, and gate levels while still executing at reasonable speed (Miranker *et al.*, 1989).

Existing commercial designs were used wherever it was felt that such components had a sufficient performance level to meet design goals. This allowed the design team to concentrate its efforts on areas where such chips were not available and on areas where the expertise of the Titan design team could make a substantial contribution to the state of the art.

Because of cost and size constraints (and the technology chosen) clock speed in the final machine would have to be limited to 16 to 20 MHz. It was clear that innovation with parallelism at all levels would be crucial to achieving good computation rates. In order to reduce design time and costs, gate arrays instead of full-custom chips were to be used for customized logic.

By June 1986 the key designers had been hired and the overall architecture settled upon. There would be from one to four vector processors in a system with a shared memory. These vector processors would be identical units and could be used for either scientific computation or floating-point computations to generate graphical displays. The performance target had risen to six MFLOPS with an intent of mounting three processors on a 16×22-inch board. By mid-June it became apparent that the design required more chips than initially anticipated and the target was dropped to two processors per board.

The compiler group had been performing a hand-analysis of several numerical benchmarks including LINPACK (Dongarra, 1989), Lawrence Livermore loops (McMahon, 1986), and selected C programs. LINPACK was selected as the benchmark most representative of the anticipated users of this machine.

The heart of LINPACK is the solution of a set of linear equations by Gaussian elimination. The basic operation in Gaussian elimination is the multiplication of one equation (X) by a scalar (A) and addition to a second equation (Y) to eliminate a variable. This operation is called DAXPY (Double Precision AX Plus Y). A special vector multiply and accumulate instruction (DVMA—Double Precision Vector Multiply and Accumulate) was specified and the architecture evolved to support execution of the DVMA instruction at the rate of one vector element result per clock tick. The floating-point ALU that had been selected was capable of eight MFLOPS. Similarly the multiplier was capable of eight MFLOPS. If both units could be kept completely occupied, the theoretical maximum performance was 16 MFLOPS, substantially exceeding the design goals. Of course, sustained performance would not be this high, a fact discussed in Chapter 7.

It quickly became apparent that a bus with extremely high bandwidth would be needed to support the peak computation rates possible with the

DVMA instruction. The heart of the design would be the buses intercon-
necting memory with the vector units, and so the summer of 1986 focused
on developing a bus. To reach the 16 million bus operations per second
required to supply the operands to the floating-point units, some key signals on the bus had to be implemented in ECL logic for speed while other
signals were implemented in TTL for lower system costs. To avoid wasted
bus cycles, resources such as memory banks would broadcast their status
on busy lines. If a resource was busy, a requester would not initiate a bus
cycle, thereby preventing wasted bus-arbitration cycles.

A detailed functional model for the bus was developed to study arbitration schemes and link conflicts which had already been observed in Cray
supercomputers. This model was required to identify conflicts that only
occurred between individual operations and were not visible in more traditional random-pattern generation simulations. While the specification
for the bus was being refined, design was started on a special ECL chip to
perform bus arbitration.

By September of 1986, the bus specification had been completed and
the backplane designed. A detailed SPICE (Nagel, 1975) circuit model was
developed for the backplane to test the integrity and quality of the analog
wave forms. Because of the critical nature of the bus, a special monitor
board was designed which could clock signals on various ports and observe
their results. The monitor board and first-pass backplane were available in
January of 1987, and experimentation with the signal quality indicated
that the SPICE models were very accurate.

By September of 1986, the relative size of the various portions of the
system had become apparent. The design-team members were grouped
into subsystem teams including two for the floating-point vector unit, two
for the integer-processing unit, two for graphics, two for memory, and one
for input/output. To make the logic fit in the prescribed board area, it was
determined that eight gate arrays had to be designed. The complexity of
the gate arrays varied considerably, as shown by the sizes listed in Table
1.1. An arbiter gate array would be used by all boards to attach to the
system bus. The interleaved memory would require three gate arrays for
the memory controllers and the cross-point switch to provide the necessary
memory bandwidth. The final four gate arrays were used in the processor
board: Kit (the "kitchen sink" chip) containing miscellaneous functions,
VDS for the Vector Data Switch, and two VCU chips for the Vector Control Unit.

1.4.2.2   THE PROCESSOR

In the fall of 1986, it became apparent that the size and complexity of the
vector unit had been underestimated. Estimates for the other portions of

TABLE 1.1.   Titan gate arrays.

Gate array	Number of Gates
Bus arbiter	2 000
Memory control A	1 600
Memory control B	4 000
Memory control C	10,000
Kit	10,000
VDS	10,000
VCU A	38,000
VCU B	43,000

the system proved to be within a factor of two of the final size, but estimates for the vector-processing unit were off by a factor of four, mostly because the complexity of the undertaking had not been fully understood by the designers at the outset. To separate the integer and floating-point units, the processor board design was divided in two. It was then decided that the processor board should first be laid out and fabricated without the floating-point hardware in order to provide an integer unit for testing with other system boards and for software development. The integer unit design was based upon a board designed by MIPS Inc., featuring the MIPS R2000 chip.

The computer-aided design tools for board placement and routing were acquired during early fall of 1986, and board layout and release commenced during the last month of 1986. Part of the way through board layout in November of 1986, it became apparent that because of limitations with the automatic printed circuit-board routing software, as well as requirements for routing space around the gate-array chips, the target had to be reduced to one processor per board.[4]

First-pass boards were completed by the board fabrication vendor in March, April, and May of 1987. The CPU, I/O, and backplane were 12-layer boards, while the memory and graphics boards required 14 layers. The backplane worked the first time power was supplied, and the processor board with the integer unit was ready to run code at speed within three hours of receipt of the board. The memory board was running diagnostics within 45 minutes of final assembly. Six of the eight gate arrays worked the first time and were shipped with the original units. The other two gate

---

[4]The initial intent had been to place chips on 0.2-inch centers with associated decoupling capacitors; however, because of routing software limitations, the chips had to be moved to 0.3-inch centers with the capacitors occupying the extra 0.1 inch between the chips. This greatly reduced the anticipated density of the boards, leading to a reduction of the goal from two processors to only one per board.

arrays had to be revised, and second-pass parts were shipped with the first product. This excellent record was achieved primarily because of extensive use of design and simulation CAD tools (Miranker *et al.*, 1989).

As designers completed their individual board designs, the entire team focused on the vector unit. The vector unit had grown to such complexity that the three SUN workstations assigned to simulation, working full time for several months, could only simulate 1/16th of a second of real time. Although simulation had previously proven very successful in producing near error-free boards, progress using simulations was too slow for the VCU. Therefore, it was decided to fabricate one of the vector control unit chips for high-speed testing. A pseudo-random number generator drove the chip inputs and helped uncover 18 design errors.

Further simulation of the vector unit continued through July and August of 1987, and a special plug-in board hosting Weitek floating-point chips was designed and fabricated as a stopgap until the vector-control unit gate-array chips were available. This board appeared in September of 1987 and provided software developers a means for testing compiled code. In July 1987, the other boards were assembled into five machines, denoted the P0 series. These systems were complete except for floating point. These five machines were converted into P1 series machines, complete with floating point, when the processor boards with the vector unit were delivered in December 1987.

The fall of 1987 focused on diagnostics and translations of the simulation scripts into diagnostic code. During this period, designers switched between tasks and performed whatever was necessary to meet the internal milestones. For example, one engineering manager spent several months writing and vectorizing graphics code so that the graphics board could be integrated with the other software portions of the system.

1.4.2.3   GRAPHICS

The basic attributes of the graphics board had been set in early 1986 to include a 50-million pixel-per-second drawing rate, pseudo-color, and full-color double buffering. The system had to be expandable so that a user could upgrade by adding extra hardware. Chips from Raster Technologies ("Raster Tech") had been selected to provide the basic graphics-rendering operations.

By November 1986, estimates were available for the size, cost, and power required for the graphics board. The board was available in June 1987, and four bugs were found in the Raster Tech chips. Two of the bugs were discovered immediately while the other two took several months to find. Over 100 wires were required to work around an incorrect assump-

tion about the video RAM chip clock and the design errors in the Raster
Tech chips. The system PROM had to be modified to support the graphics.
    The graphics board was simulated in Verilog. However, there were no
Verilog models available for the Raster Tech chips. An interface to the
Raster Tech chips was modeled according to the specifications provided
by Raster Tech. The bus interface was simulated in Verilog. Since the interface was defined in programmable logic arrays, the PAL equations were
directly translated into a Verilog model. Thus, the simulation was able to
support the CPU issuing commands to the graphics board across the
backplane.
    From the last quarter of 1986 through the availability of the P0
machines, hardware design worked with manufacturing to select and qualify components and peripherals. The P0 machines were used in Strife testing to evaluate the maturity of the design (see the subsection on Quality
below).

1.4.3   OPERATING SYSTEM

During the early system planning, it was decided that Titan would be a
symmetric multiprocessor with multiprocessor features carried to the user
level. At the time, AT&T was moving from Unix System version V.2 to
version V.3, which included many enhancements such as the concept of
streams. However, version V.3 had no support for local area networks.
One of the first decisions was whether local area network support should
be copied from Berkeley Unix or whether Stardent should use streams to
support TCP/IP. The decision was made to proceed with the second
approach. However, TCP/IP using streams had several potential pitfalls.
Common buffer pools were used for all protocol managers, introducing
the possibility for deadlocks. Streams also made assumptions that tran-
scended software module boundaries. One such assumption was buffer
size. As messages were encapsulated multiple times by streams, it became
possible to lose the message boundary and consequently the control byte
at the head of the message.
    It was also decided that C shells for job control from Berkeley Unix
should be supported. The Berkeley Unix libraries would be ported so that
Berkeley code could be compiled, linked in with the appropriate library,
and executed. However there were many differences between the Berkeley
Unix tools and Unix System V.3.
    A key issue was the focus on how to debug parallel programs—whether
they be user programs or kernel programs. In particular, break points had
to be made to work in a parallel environment. A symbolic debugger which
could be booted over the network and which contained knowledge of the

disk file structures was contained in PROM. Because the compiler was highly optimizing and could allocate even global variables to registers, substantial work had to be performed on the symbol table to make this information available to the debugger. The concept of threads was developed to eliminate system-call overhead. Idle threads could spin on a semaphore with little cost, because Titan was a single-user workstation which was optimized for performance instead of throughput.

Designing system synchronization primitives was also a major undertaking. Identification of races and double-locking of the same semaphore were important for debugging. Many bugs were flushed out on code running on only a single processor.

The port of Unix to the MIPS chip executing in a single processor provided by MIPS Inc., started in June of 1986 and was completed by September. The MIPS chips had two deficiencies: the physical memory space was not contiguous, and the existing Unix kernel software did not conform to hardware word-alignment-addressing constraints. Resolving both of these problems required modifications to the Unix kernel. Each time the operating system was ported to new hardware (which was done three times to different hardware revisions before first customer shipment), a period of approximately six weeks of intense debugging was required to identify new problems. Porting of the operating system to the P0 hardware yielded a login prompt in multi-user mode in June 1987. Compilation of the kernel on the P0 hardware led to numerous core dumps. These were traced to a bug in the MIPS chip and were fixed by having the compiler generate a NOP at the end of every 4096 byte page. A similar period of intense debugging occurred in December 1987 when the vector unit became available. By February 1988 the operating system was considered stable.

1.4.4   COMPILER

An ideal way to develop a compiler in conjunction with a hardware design is to iterate back and forth between hardware and compiler as was done several times by AT&T during the 1970s. The performance of the code produced by the compiler is analyzed, and those hardware features that are not utilized by the compiler can be subtracted by the hardware-design team. Those features that are extensively used by the compiler can be made to run faster by the hardware designers. If, on the other hand, the compiler is producing constructs that are costly to implement in hardware, the hardware designers could request modifications to the code generator and the replacement of code templates by easier-to-implement features. This ideal software/hardware development cycle is shown in Figure 1.5.

The luxury of repeated compiler/hardware iterations is not available in

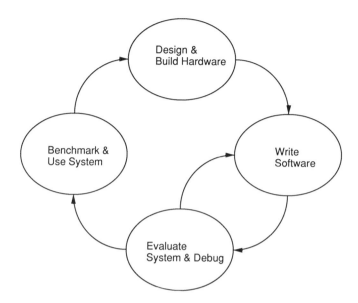

FIGURE 1.5.   An ideal hardware/software development cycle.

a start-up company that has no existing architecture and that must get to market quickly. Thus the early compiler work consisted of substantial hand analysis of key benchmarks such as LINPACK, Livermore Loops, and some C programs. Substantial work had already been done by others on vectorizing standard codes such as FORTRAN. The real challenge was going to be parallel processing for which there had been very little previous work performed.

A key to the production of parallel code is synchronization. A study was made of synchronization mechanisms and a specification written as to what would be supported in hardware and software. Some synchronization approaches were rejected, since they would be produced for every FORTRAN loop and thus would represent a severe penalty. The problem was aggravated by the fact that the MIPS chip did not provide a test and set instruction for synchronization. A synchronization mechanism (Load-and-Sync) had to be built into the memory system.

The compiler was designed with the intent to handle both vectors and parallel code. Because the requirements of Titan were perceived as being very different from the requirements of the uniprocessor systems provided by MIPS, the compiler work was started from scratch. In essence, it was as if three compilers were built: a scalar/vector compiler, a parallel compiler, and a performance-tuned compiler. Often, the performance was not understood until the actual hardware was available. The key was understanding the memory-reference patterns and how interference occurred between them. In particular, the most difficult part was identifying the bottlenecks. A bottleneck could be in different regions of the system, depending on the actual code generated. For example, the bottleneck could be in loading the vector registers, in performing the vector operations, or in the memory bandwidth. A detailed cycle-by-cycle analysis of where the time was spent was performed so that heuristics could be built to guide the compiler. In order to understand these relationships fully, the actual hardware was required.

The compiler was built and simulated on the MIPS processor to ensure correctness of the semantics; however, this was not useful for establishing performance estimates. The Titan implementation had different time constants for the various functions. In particular, synchronization between the integer and floating-point units took far longer than anticipated. The compiler had put synchronization in the inner loops of the code. Information was available in the vectorizer that demonstrated that these synchronization points were unnecessary. Thus, commencing in December 1987, the compiler was torn apart and put back together in order to make this information more readily available to the code generators.

This reworking of the compiler led to several months of compiler instability until the design errors could be removed. There are over 340,000 lines of FORTRAN regression test programs that are run on the compiler every time a change is made. These tests had to be written from scratch because no systematic body of tests could be found or bought.

Discovering bugs is particularly difficult in a vectorizing/parallelizing compiler because user code is transformed at least half a dozen times into various intermediate forms so that small changes of source code may trigger wide variations in internal form. Because bugs usually occur at "boundary" conditions (e.g., just running out of registers), it is difficult to generate architecturally-independent test cases.

Because of the analysis and compiler tuning, improvements of a factor of 5 to 10 occurred in compiler-generated programs during the last half of 1988. In particular, the Stardent team began to respect the Lawrence Livermore Loops benchmark, which reports performance as a harmonic mean (for a discussion of the importance of using the harmonic mean, see [Smith, 1988]). Use of the harmonic mean focuses attention on the slowest performer. Customers are sensitive to the slowest portion of their code, and a poor performer can swamp out any gains in other portions of the system. The use of harmonic means forced the math functions and graphics functions to be recoded and hand-optimized so that optimization efforts were uniformly applied to all aspects of performance.

1.4.5 QUALITY

In April of 1986, the Stardent founders issued a statement on their commitment to quality: "Our principal goal is to be a quality company, quality as measured by our people, products, operation, and manner of doing business. The commitment to uncompromising quality is the cornerstone of our culture." The intent was to manage quality from the beginning rather than attempt to add it after the fact. A primary focus was on prevention of problems and their permanent correction.

There are four phases to quality assurance as applied to the hardware development process: component selection, design verification, manufacturing process, and system assembly. The first members of the quality team were hired almost two years prior to the first shipment of products to customers. Quality was to be designed and manufactured in. From their experiences with other companies, the design engineers felt a personal responsibility for the final quality of their product.

Quality started with the component vendors. The primary selection criterion for a vendor was quality. During the vendor-qualification process, Stardent worked with the vendor to establish quality specifications and procedures such as those for component burn-in. The component purchasing contract had clauses specifying burn-in, statistical product control, and liability for failure to meet contract goals. In several cases, vendor education was required to meet the contractual specifications.

During the fall of 1987 a design verification test (DVT) was set up for the first Stardent-constructed prototypes to determine the maturity of the design. Strife testing, a combination of stress and life testing, was used to accelerate any failure modes. The design was tested beyond its specified limits. For example, the specification called for ambient temperatures ranging from $-10°C$ to $50°C$. The Strife test was conducted from $-20°C$ to $60°C$. The actual Strife test used the "eight-corner" testing method, testing in each of the eight combinations of temperature (-20 to $60°C$), voltage (4.75 V to 5.25 V on the 5-volt supply), and frequency (15.2 to 16.8 MHz).

If the systems can operate correctly in regions beyond their specifications, there is a degree of margin built into the design. Any errors that were encountered were carefully considered to determine whether they were due to hardware or software. A few problems during Strife testing were found in the peripherals, but these were corrected by the peripheral vendors.

The manufacturing process was designed by representatives from manufacturing, production, test, quality, and materials engineering. Because of the stringent vendor-qualification process, components are considered defect-free upon arrival at the manufacturing facility. The boards are first placed in in-circuit testers for removal of any manufacturing defects. Subsequently the boards are tested functionally and are finally burned in for 96 hours with power and temperature cycling. The board-testing process was developed in the United States and subsequently transferred to Kubota, Stardent's Japanese manufacturing partner.

Kubota produced its first prototype boards in the spring of 1988 and shipped them to Stardent for qualification. This first batch of boards had a yield of greater than 50%, which was good for complex boards of over 500 components and 360 square inches of board area. Goals for in-circuit testing yields rose from 70% to 80% and functional testing from 80% to 95%. Yields for the printed circuit boards were projected at 90%. All of these goals have been met and exceeded. Stardent worked with Kubota to qualify the vendors supplying Kubota as well as to qualify Kubota's manufacturing process.

Final assembly and test of the systems is done by Stardent. All peripherals are 100% tested prior to installation in the system. The system, in the customer's intended configuration, is burned in for 72 hours at 40°C. Figure 1.6 depicts the cycling for burn-in of a board with temperature cycling,

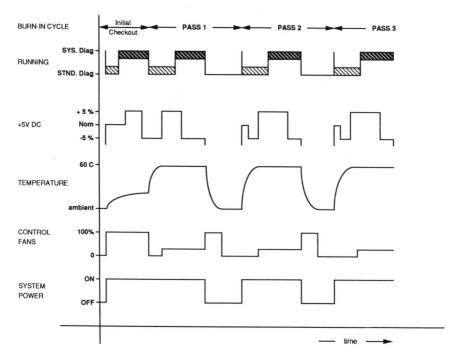

FIGURE 1.6.   Typical burn-in profile.

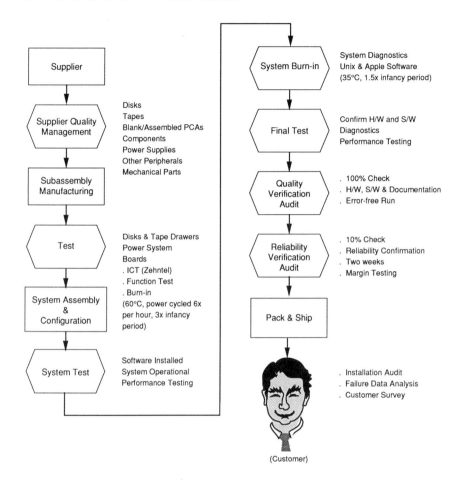

FIGURE 1.7. Manufacturing process flow.

power margins, power cycling, air flow, and diagnostic variations. Both the board-level burn-in and system-level burn-in have to be error-free before the system is shipped.

The first demonstration units were released to the field in April of 1988, and it was not until July 1988 that the first field failure occurred in a population of over 20 machines. This failure was due to a design defect which was not caught during the design verification test. An added component removed this defect. From an initial goal of a 2000-hour mean time to failure, a demonstrated field mean time to failure of over 10,000 hours was accomplished within the first six months of first customer shipment.

The first non-random failure in the field occurred in October of 1988 when nine machines were damaged in shipping. The origin of the problem lay with rough handling by shippers of the individual pallets for the machine and accessories box. The solution was simply to bolt the two pallets together to make a larger object which was more difficult to tip over. The problem and solution were found in only one day.

Figure 1.7 depicts the flow of components to final assembled machines and the various quality checks along the way.

The key aspects of quality for Stardent can be summarized as follows:

- Company management commitment to quality.
- Quality of the design team and their dedication to designing quality into their product.
- Hiring of experienced quality manufacturing talent.
- Teaming up with a Japanese company to bring Japanese excellence in manufacturing to bear on printed circuit-board production.
- Supplier selection based on quality.
- Qualification of vendor components.
- Strife testing of the design to demonstrate margin.
- Quality designed into the manufacturing process and utilization of burn-in.
- A data collection system which tracks all problems until they are resolved.

1.5   THE NEXT GENERATION

The focus of this book will be the first generation of Titan, consisting of the P0, P1, and P2 versions of the machine. The Titan P3 will be discussed in Chapter 7. The P3 machine resolves many of the system performance and balance problems that were visible only after extended use of the initial machine. But first, Chapter 2 presents a tutorial on the various techniques used in the Titan architecture to enhance performance.

ARCHITECTURAL EVOLUTION—
ISSUES AND SOLUTIONS IN HIGH-
PERFORMANCE DESIGN

It is important not only to understand how a machine like Titan is constructed, but also why it is built the way it is. Knowledge of the design tradeoffs involved in creating a high-performance architecture is important to understanding its strengths and weaknesses.

In this chapter, we shall explore the chain of refinements that leads from a simple uniprocessor to the high-performance architecture used by vector supercomputers such as Titan. We shall start by reviewing uniprocessor limitations and then examine a sequence of improvement strategies that ultimately lead to the Titan architecture.

Specific improvement strategies that may be made over uniprocessors include the use of memory performance hierarchies, speedup through specialization, speedup through overlapping operations (concurrency in time), speedup through replicating function units (concurrency in space), and use of vector operations.

2.1 IN THE BEGINNING: UNIPROCESSORS

Computers were invented when calculators were combined with a modifiable memory to store sequences of operations. Three separate functions were identified in the earliest days of the stored-program computer. As depicted in Figure 2.1 these consisted of:

- Processor—Fetches and executes instructions stored in memory.
- Memory—Contains both instructions and data.
- Input/Output—For communication with humans and other computers.

In a common configuration, the functional units were attached to a bus as an interconnection structure.

Programs composed of a sequence of instructions for the processor were loaded into the main memory through the input hardware. Data for the program to operate on were similarly loaded. Instructions were executed one at a time until the program was finished. After execution of the program, results stored in main memory were available as input to another program or communicated externally through the output hardware.

In classical uniprocessors, there is no overlapping of operations. Each instruction is fetched and completely executed before the next instruction is fetched. This mode of sequential execution (i.e., the sequential instruction fetch/data-fetch/execute/data-store cycle) can severely limit the instruction execution rate of a processor.

2.1.1   UNIPROCESSOR LIMITS

An implementation of a classical uniprocessor structure is inherently limited in growth potential. The processor's performance is fixed, and main memory performance can only be varied over a small range. Furthermore, the sequential instruction execution inherent in a classical uniprocessor

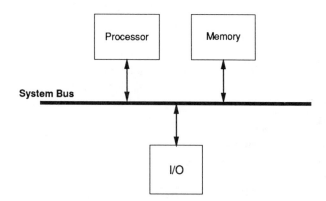

FIGURE 2.1.   Classical single bus style of connection.

limits performance improvements to just those obtainable through improved electronic circuits.

Uniprocessors have improved dramatically in speed over the years. Technological advances have produced significantly higher circuit speeds with a factor of four increase in the last decade for bipolar technology (yielding a compounded growth rate of 15% per year). However, there are indications that circuit designers will reach fundamental physical limits (i.e., speed of light and atomic dimensions) by the year 2000.

As these limits to uniprocessor performance are approached, it will become more and more difficult to increase processor performance through circuit technology alone. Also, to utilize these speed improvements often requires a completely new design, potentially preventing older application software from benefiting from the new technology.

An equally important consideration is that, based on historical trends, the demand for computational power will probably always exceed the supply. Therefore, some means of improving the sequential execution model of the classical uniprocessor is very important.

2.1.2   BREAKING THE LIMITS OF THE UNIPROCESSOR

Since the inception of the electronic digital computer, users have sought higher performance. Computer designers can diminish the performance limitations of current technology by exploiting a wide array of techniques including memory hierarchies, specialization of hardware, concurrency through overlap, concurrency through replication, and use of vector operations.

Initially, some of these performance-improvement techniques (especially memory hierarchies and hardware specialization) were applied to uniprocessor designs to improve performance of existing design families. However, the same inherent limit to uniprocessors applies no matter how exotic the architecture: only a small constant number of instructions (typically one) may be issued per clock cycle. This bottleneck is called the Flynn Limit (Flynn, 1966).[5]

In order to break the instruction-issuing bottleneck, more than one processor must be used to introduce concurrency through replication of processors. The number of operations that are allowed to happen simultaneously determines the degree of concurrency. In general, the larger the

---

[5] A special case is the Very Large Instruction Word class of computer, in which a number of execution units are handled by the same control unit. This is an approach that takes advantage of a loophole in the Flynn Limit by compacting several different operations into one very long instruction word.

degree of concurrency, the larger the increase in speed over a sequential (non-concurrent) design.

The use of multiple processors in a system greatly affects the design of other aspects of the system (notably the memory hierarchy). Therefore, in the following sections we shall describe improvements with an eye to final incorporation in a multiple processor system.

2.2 MEMORY PERFORMANCE HIERARCHIES

Historically, memory cost has increased with increasing memory speed; usually, memory density has also decreased with increasing memory. Thus, there is a tradeoff of cost, speed, and density among storage technologies. The various types of memory available (e.g., magnetic disk, dynamic RAMs, high-speed static RAMs) form a spectrum of available cost/performance tradeoffs.

In order to exploit the availability of different cost/performance options, computer architects make use of the concept of locality. A program is said to exhibit locality when the memory-access patterns display some cohesiveness over relatively short periods of time.

Locality in time (called temporal locality) is a program's tendency to access a segment of memory repeatedly in a short period of time. For example, a program loop repeatedly executes the instructions within the loop in a relatively short time span. In terms of program-data access, locality in time refers to the fact that some variables (say loop counters) are accessed more frequently than others.

Locality in space (called spatial locality) is a program's tendency to access data that lies close together in memory. For example, most instructions are not branches, meaning that if a particular instruction is fetched from memory for execution, it is likely that the instruction after it will be fetched next.

Memory-performance hierarchies are based on the principle that slower memory is less expensive than fast memory and that the locality of programs may be captured in small amounts of high-speed memory for use by the processor. The small portion of memory that is actually accessed over a short period of time is called the *working set* (Denning, 1970).

In most hierarchies this principle is taken even further by providing different levels of increasingly faster (and smaller) blocks of memory. Memory segments that are close to the processor are fast and small and hold a working set for a very short period of program execution. As memory segments get further from the processor in the hierarchy, they get larger and are thus able to hold working sets for longer periods of execution time, but with reduced access speed. Capturing the working set into a small piece of high-speed memory may be done by software, hardware, or both.

Figure 2.2 shows a typical memory hierarchy described both in terms of the devices used to implement the memory and the use of the memory within the system. At the peak of the pyramid are the CPU registers, which are the fastest, smallest (because of limited on-chip space), and most expensive (per bit of storage) devices used in a computer. Next is cache memory, which is usually constructed from static RAM chips. Below that is physical memory, or just plain "memory" as seen by the user, which is typically constructed from dynamic RAM chips. Below that is virtual memory for holding the overflow of physical memory, which is most often magnetic disk (but may also be dynamic RAM chips or other devices). Underneath these layers are support layers that hold non-executing programs for long term online storage and archival off-line storage. The access times and costs are, of course, sensitive to technological advance and the economics of the system represented but are nonetheless generally representative of those seen in practice.

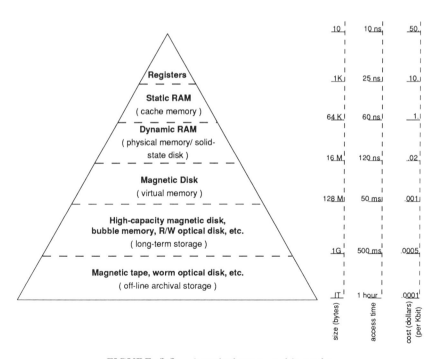

FIGURE 2.2.   A typical memory hierarchy.

2.2.1   REGISTER SETS

The most obvious and almost universally used method for speeding up the apparent access time to memory is to use a set of registers in the CPU to hold frequently accessed values. Because the registers are built of the same technology as the CPU, they may be accessed at full speed by the processor. This access speed is typically once or twice (a read followed by a write) in each clock cycle. In microprocessors, these registers have the added advantage that they reside on the same chip as the processor, increasing the speed of access possible over memory that resides off-chip.

Registers are a software-managed portion of the memory hierarchy. Compilers must explicitly indicate data transfer to and from other memory by using load and store instructions. They do have an advantage over other (hardware) hierarchy management schemes because the compiler has knowledge of future operations; this knowledge may be used to load the registers optimally with needed values, knowing which values will be needed when. This places an extra burden on the compiler, but the extra effort is usually rewarded with significant performance gains.

Examples of register set usage in Titan, shown in Figure 2.3, include the 32 registers used inside the MIPS chips, and the 8096-element Vector Register File used in the Titan VPU. In both cases, data must be moved into these registers before it may be operated upon by instructions. The compiler arranges for the register sets to retain values that will be used soon while transferring results that will not be reused back to memory.

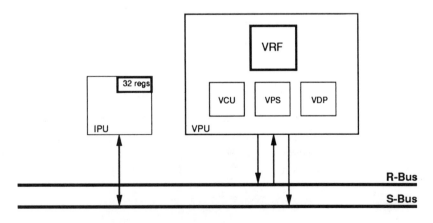

FIGURE 2.3.   Register set usage in Titan.

2.2.2   CACHE MEMORY PRINCIPLES

If CPU registers are considered the peak of the memory performance hierarchy, then cache memory is the second tier. In contrast to registers, cache memory is designed to be an automatically allocated resource controlled by hardware; its existence is, to a large degree, invisible to the executing program.

The theory of operation of cache memory is that a special hardware controller can automatically exploit the locality inherent in program and data-memory accesses. It does this by retaining the most recent words of data accessed by the processor in a special high-speed memory—the cache memory. Because programs exhibit temporal locality, it is likely that once a piece of data has been accessed, it will be accessed again soon. The cache hardware controller stores accessed memory values in the cache memory so that the second and subsequent accesses refer to fast cache memory instead of slow physical memory, speeding up the average access time.

Of course, there soon comes a time when the cache memory is full. This leads to a variety of strategies for deciding which piece of data to remove from the cache memory before loading the new data. Strategies include first-in/first-out, least recently used, and random replacement.

2.2.2.1   *REVIEW OF CACHE TERMINOLOGY AND TRADEOFFS*

Consider the following simple model. Let h be the cache "hit ratio," the probability that an addressed word is in the cache. If $t.fetch$ is the average time to fetch an instruction or operand, $t.cache$ is the cache access time, and $t.mem$ is the memory access time (composed of both bus and memory delays), then

$$t.fetch = h * t.cache + (1 - h) * t.mem$$

and

$$\text{peak access rate} = \frac{1}{t.fetch}$$

If $h = 1$, then all memory requests are in cache and the memory system responds to all accesses at cache speed. At the other extreme, if $h = 0$, the cache makes no improvement to system performance.

Figure 2.4 illustrates a typical set-associative cache showing the major parameters in cache design: cache capacity, block size, and set size.

The *cache capacity* is the maximum number of memory words that can be resident in the cache. It corresponds to the size and number of memory chips used to implement the cache. A large cache size is desirable, since

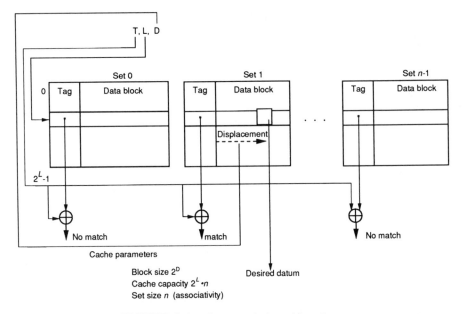

FIGURE 2.4.   Set associative addressing.

the larger the cache size, the more likely it is that a given entry will still be resident in the cache when it is referenced a second time. In general, the bigger the cache size, the better the cache performance.

The *block size* (sometimes called the line size) is the number of words stored as a group with the same tag in the cache memory. Since each block of cache must have associated with it some address information (the tag), having a large block size decreases the relative overhead of tag storage by increasing the number of bytes stored in cache for a given tag. Common block sizes are one or two machine words (4 or 8 bytes). A large block size takes advantage of spatial locality within programs (the tendency of a program to make memory references to adjacent addresses). However, too large a block size can waste memory bandwidth by causing words that are never accessed to be loaded into cache.

The *set size* (associativity) is the number of blocks in the cache that can have the same index. In a direct-mapped cache (set size of 1), every memory address maps into one and only one cache location, typically specified by a group of the lower bits of the memory address. In a two-way set-associative cache, every memory address maps into a pair of entries (with the pair determined by the lowest few bits of the memory address, and the set entry within the pair determined by the replacement policy—least recently used, first-in/first-out, or random). In an N-way set-associative cache, every memory address maps into a set of N entries. In general, a larger set size reduces the possibility of thrashing if multiple frequently used memory locations happen to map to the same set. On the other hand, a multi-way set-associative cache is more complex to build and tends to be slower than direct-mapped cache.

The hardware separates the processor address into three fields: tag, index, and displacement. The index field is used to access N sets of tables simultaneously (where N is the set size). Each of the N tables simultaneously compares its tag field contents with the tag fields specified by the address. If there is a match, a hit occurs and the index is used to select a block while the displacement selects a word from within the block. If there is no match, the instruction or data must be retrieved from memory. Cache hit ratio h is a complex function of the cache parameters and applications-program behavior.

Economics dictates that the cache capacity be as small as possible while attaining the desired performance. There is a classical engineering tradeoff over block size. The larger the block, the less frequently memory has to be accessed, but too large a block size for fixed cache capacity decreases the number of blocks resident in cache and hence the probability of finding a datum or nonsequentially referenced instruction in the cache.

A similar tradeoff exists over set size. Historically, cache hit ratios have been determined experimentally by simulating address traces produced by application programs with various cache organizations. In general, instructions prefer "deep" and "narrow" caches—that is, those with a large index field and a small set size. Because instruction accesses are typically sequential in nature, one would like to have the cache capture the largest possible sequential set of addresses. On the other hand, data accesses are more random. Thus data prefers "shallow" and "wide" caches—that is, those with a small index field and a high degree of set associativity.

Figure 2.5 shows the placement of cache memories in Titan. There are two caches in the IPU, one for instructions and one for data. In addition, Titan uses a cache memory for the Translation Lookaside Buffer (explained later) in the VPU.

It is important to note that Titan does not use a cache memory for data for the VPU, instead relying only on the compiler-managed registers in the VRF for fast-access data storage. Titan avoids the use of cache for the VPU because, along with its potential benefits, cache brings with it some limitations. The limitation at issue here is that if too many data accesses are performed between accessing a single element twice, the entire cache may be swept clean, resulting in a 0% hit rate. In these cases, cache provides no performance increase and may even decrease performance while a compiler-controlled register file can deliver a very good performance increase.

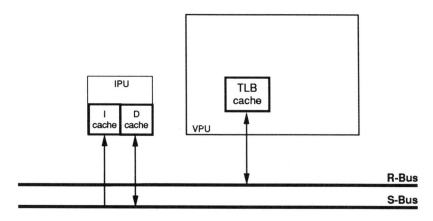

FIGURE 2.5.   Cache usage in Titan.

2.2.2.2   *MULTIPROCESSOR CACHE COHERENCY*

An important consideration in multiprocessors is maintaining consistent and correct copies of data across multiple caches throughout a system. The problem arises if two processors attempt to change the same variable in memory, a common operation for communication between two processes in the system. If one processor only makes a change in its cache memory, the other processor will not see the results of that change and will make its own copy of the old value. This results in several different values for the same variable existing simultaneously in scattered parts of the system. This is called the cache coherency problem, illustrated in Example 2.1.

Titan uses a simple write-through mechanism with invalidation for its IPU caches. Since most programs do not modify their own instructions (or at least are not supposed to modify them), only the IPU D-cache has bus-watching logic to detect write operations and invalidate D-cache words that have been modified by other processors.

Because the register level of the memory hierarchy does not have a direct mapping onto memory address, no automatic hardware coherency enforcement is possible. This places the burden for ensuring safe program operation on the compiler (and ultimately the user) with respect to values kept in IPU registers and in the VPU's VRF. Also, the compiler must ensure consistency of IPU registers and VRF contents between different processors as well as within a single processor.

2.2.3   VIRTUAL MEMORY PRINCIPLES

It is often the case, especially in large scientific application programs, that the combination of a program and its data set (especially the data set) is

EXAMPLE 2.1. The cache coherency problem.

As a simple example of a cache coherency problem, consider a locking flag that is kept in an integer variable that is shared among several processes. If the flag is zero, a shared resource is free. If it is non-zero, then the resource is busy and a process desiring the resource must wait. Now, if a CPU reads the locking flag variable from memory and finds it to be non-zero, it may use a short loop to continually test the value, waiting for it to become zero (such a loop is called a spin-lock). Because the variable has been loaded into the processor's cache, it will never be read from main memory again, even if another processor changes the variable to a zero value. Thus, we have a situation where the same variable corresponding to a single memory location has two values simultaneously: a zero value in memory and a non-zero value in a cache.

A simple solution to this problem is the use of a write-through cache that performs a write to program memory whenever a variable is changed, combined with logic on each cache that watches for bus writes and invalidates any cached data value if a write to the corresponding address is observed on the bus. Other more complex schemes involving delayed write-backs combined with various word invalidation broadcast mechanisms are also possible and in use (Goodman, 1983).

too large to fit into physical memory. This problem is aggravated by having multiple programs and users sharing the same machine, especially when each user's program insists at starting at the same convenient memory location, such as address 0.

Virtual memory is used to solve these problems. Virtual memory is a mapping technique that transforms a program's logical memory address into an actual address in physical memory. A translation table that translates the program's (virtual) addresses into memory (physical) addresses is used to retain information about this mapping.

The translation table can also indicate that a particular memory block is not resident in physical memory. The operating system is invoked via a trap if such a block is used and retrieves a copy from magnetic disk. Thus, another element of the memory hierarchy is incorporated by virtual memory. The principle of operation is very similar to that of cache memory: only the working set of the program resides in physical memory while unused portions of a program are migrated to disk by operating system software as they get stale. A further advantage of using virtual memory is that programs do not have to rely on a certain amount of physical memory being installed on the machine, so the hardware configuration may change without requiring a change for programs that would not fit entirely in physical memory.

Because the translation table is accessed on each memory reference, a portion of it is often kept in a special associative memory called a Translation Lookaside Buffer (TLB). This is a high-speed cache memory that holds mapping information.

Titan uses a TLB in the VPU (called the External TLB or ETLB) as well as a TLB in the IPU. Separate TLBs with different sizes and characteristics are used to account for the different typical usages of memory by the IPU and VPU and to allow concurrent operation of the IPU and VPU.

2.3   SPEEDUP THROUGH SPECIALIZATION

Speedup through specialization involves using special-purpose hardware to accomplish frequently needed operations which are inefficiently executed by general-purpose processor hardware. The classic example of speedup through specialization is the use of floating-point acceleration hardware such as a floating-point adder to speed up operation as compared with a processor synthesizing floating-point operations from a long sequence of integer instructions.

In the most straightforward implementations of specialized hardware, only one portion of the processor is active at any given time. A good example of this might be an external floating-point coprocessor attached to an integer processor to speed up floating-point operations, as shown in Figure 2.6. In this arrangement, floating-point operation instructions halt the CPU and transfer control to the floating-point coprocessor, which performs the actual computation. When the computation is completed, control returns to the integer CPU. This has the effect of providing a CPU which seems to have built-in, high-speed, floating-point support without actually including the floating-point hardware within the CPU.

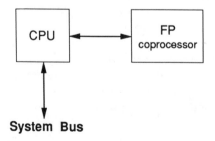

FIGURE 2.6.   CPU with floating-point coprocessor.

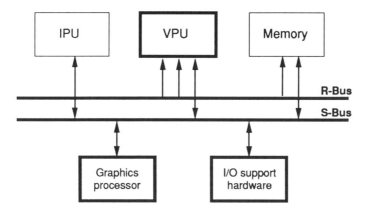

FIGURE 2.7.   Hardware specialization in Titan.

Titan makes extensive use of specialized hardware to increase program execution speed as shown in Figure 2.7. Major specialized hardware support is provided for floating point computations (hardware floating point ALU, multiplier, and divider), graphics manipulations (support for hardware line drawing and triangle drawing), and I/O operations (support for block transfers to and from I/O devices).

2.4   CONCURRENCY THROUGH OVERLAP OF OPERATIONS

No matter how much hardware budget is available for increasing the average speed of the memory hierarchy response time or for increasing the amount and complexity of specialized hardware support, eventually every uniprocessor will reach a limit. In most cases, diminishing returns from the previously described techniques will make excessive expenditures nonproductive.

The next step in increasing performance must then be to achieve concurrency of operations to allow more than one section of the hardware to be used at a time. There are two major ways to accomplish concurrent program execution: concurrency through overlap of operations (concurrency in time), and concurrency through replication (concurrency in space). Overlap allows phases of different computations which use separate resources to execute concurrently. Replication provides multiple copies of the same resource so that several sections of the same computation can proceed concurrently.

Concurrency through overlap can range from the very simple to the baroque. The major principles often employed are those of buffering and pipelining.

2.4.1   BUFFERING

2.4.1.1   IPU/FPU BUFFERING

The principal technique for overlapping activities is to provide a buffer between functional units. The buffer allows the two units to proceed at their own pace and provides a point where they can synchronize their concurrent activities. For instance, in the previous example shown in Figure 2.6, instead of having the CPU wait for the FPU to finish, the CPU could proceed with other integer computations. The only problem is that the CPU would have to be ready to accept the FPU results as soon as they were done and the FPU might have to then wait for more work to do.

In this example, the efficiency of both the CPU and the FPU may be improved by adding buffers between them as shown in Figure 2.8. This, the simplest form of buffer synchronization, is known as the producer/consumer process. In this example, there are two buffers and so two producer/consumer pairs. In the upper buffer, the CPU produces instructions and the FPU consumes them. In the lower buffer, the FPU produces results that the CPU consumes. With this arrangement, the CPU may generate as many FPU operations as possible without waiting for the FPU to complete computations (up to the limit of the buffer size) and then go on to other integer computations. When the FPU has completed an operation, it may simply place the result into the returning buffer to the CPU for use by the CPU when desired.

The value of the buffering is that not only is exact cycle-by-cycle choreography of the interchanges between the CPU and FPU avoided, but both

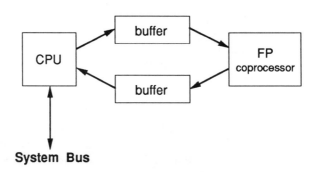

FIGURE 2.8.   CPU with buffered floating-point coprocessor.

the CPU and FPU may do as much work as possible with a minimum of interaction.

2.4.1.2 INSTRUCTION PREFETCHING

The earliest form of concurrency sought to overlap the operations of the three basic functions of processor, memory, and input/output (I/O) shown in Figure 2.1. This is accomplished by using an instruction buffer. Figure 2.9 depicts the addition of a one-instruction buffer between the processor and memory. The memory "produces" instructions for the processor to consume.

Figure 2.10 depicts the typical time sequence phases in executing an instruction. Some phases require only the processor hardware (e.g., instruction decode, instruction execution) while others require the memory and system bus (e.g., instruction fetch, operand fetch). By placing an instruction buffer between the processor and memory, the two subsystems can proceed independently. As shown in Figure 2.10, the memory could be used to fetch the next sequential address and place it in the instruction buffer, while the processor decoded and executed the current instruction. If the memory were always faster than the processor and if all instructions were executed in sequence, then except for a start-up transient, the time to fetch an instruction would be completely overlapped with the time to execute instructions.

It is generally impossible to guarantee that the memory will always complete before the processor or vice versa. Thus the consumer (i.e., the processor) must check the instruction buffer for valid data prior to proceeding. If the buffer is empty, the processor must wait. If the buffer is full,

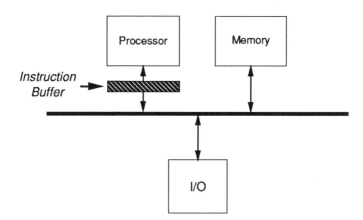

FIGURE 2.9. Use of an instruction buffer.

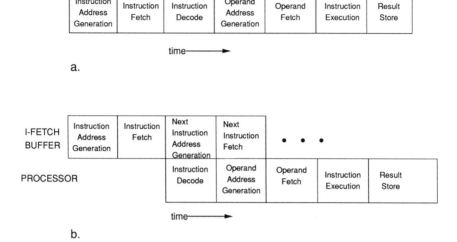

FIGURE 2.10.   Instruction execution phases. (a) Typical instruction execution phases. (b) Instruction execution phases with instruction fetch buffer.

the processor consumes the instruction and marks the buffer empty. The memory behaves exactly opposite. If the buffer is full, it suspends instruction prefetching and waits. If the buffer is empty, it prefetches the next instruction.

It is possible to prefetch more than the next single incoming instruction. This can be done by providing an instruction prefetch buffer greater in size than a single instruction. Like cache memories, instruction prefetch buffers dynamically attempt to capture locality. If a program has good spatial locality, then prefetched instruction will have a high probability of being executed.

There are many places that the addition of buffers and their associated control logic can provide speedup through concurrency. For example, the first computers and modern small computers employed the processor to control I/O and hence could not perform I/O concurrently with other processing. Because the speed differential between electronic and mechanical technologies was two orders of magnitude, the processor was inefficiently utilized. When a small amount of logic was added to the I/O device, the processor only had to start the I/O operation and then continue non-I/O processing. When the I/O device finished, it would notify the processor by means of an interrupt. This allowed the data for one job to be loaded while a second executed and the results from a third job were printed. In the ideal case three times as many jobs could be processed by a given computer (batch mode) as before.

The effect of concurrency on software varies from none to a need for totally new programming styles, compilers, operating systems, debuggers, library support, and application programs. Instruction prefetch and inter-leaved memory are two examples of hardware concurrency that are totally transparent to the software. Some concurrency techniques impact only the operating system (e.g., processor-I/O overlap) or impact user software in minor ways (e.g., in the imprecise interrupts in the IBM System/360 Model 91 (Siewiorek *et al.*, 1982)). At the other extreme, concurrency structures may not only require dedicated programming, but also require entirely new algorithms (as do associative and systolic array processors, for exam-ple). In general, only designs that do not require major rewriting of appli-cation programs are acceptable for general-purpose computing. The impact can be lessened by the use of sophisticated compilers that hide the details of the hardware requirements from the user.

Titan uses several different buffers for its operation, as shown in Figure 2.11. The IPU uses its cache memory as a read buffer by using a line size of two words so that a second word adjacent to the word being loaded into

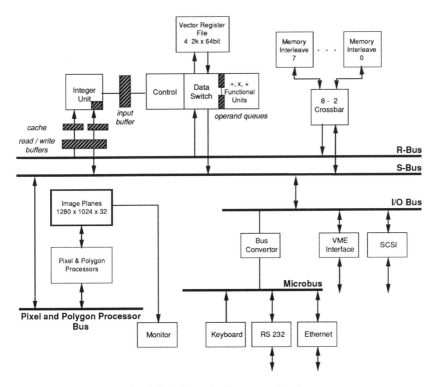

FIGURE 2.11.   Buffer usage in Titan.

cache is fetched on even-word-addressed memory misses. For instruction fetches, this means that an instruction fetch reads the instruction being fetched as well as the next instruction into cache at the same time, providing an instruction prefetch function. The IPU itself performs overlapped instruction fetching and execution to start the cache read process while the previous instruction is still executing. The IPU also has a write buffer to allow the IPU to proceed without waiting for a written value to be transferred to memory.

Titan uses a buffer between the IPU and the VPU to transfer instructions generated by the IPU to the VPU control logic. Within the VPU, the Vector Data Switch (VDS) provides buffers for transferring information among resources.

Titan's VRF may be considered a buffer also, because operands are read into the VRF before being operated on by the Vector Data Path. To the extent that the VPU is able to chain consecutive loads and vector operations, and vector operations with stores, the VRF actually acts as a buffer between the VDP and memory. To some extent, the IPU registers may be thought of as a compiler-managed operand buffer as well.

Finally, Titan's GPU uses three buffers. It has an image plane that is a buffered copy of the graphic image being displayed on the monitor, as well as a Z-buffer used to contain depth-sorting information. Additionally, it uses the memory subsystem for a buffer to hold instruction lists that are built by the IPU and then executed by the VPU.

2.4.2 PIPELINING

Pipelining involves the breaking down of a process into small steps and then executing the steps in parallel on different data in a production-line fashion. To see how this works, let us continue the discussion of the instruction-fetching buffer from the previous section.

The overlap between the memory and processor as depicted in Figure 2.12 is reminiscent of an automobile assembly line where each station adds something to the automobile and passes the product on to the next stage. Raw material enters at one end of the assembly line, and every minute a car is driven off the other end of the "line." The throughput is thus one car per minute, but the time to convert raw material to a completed product is about eight hours (the latency). This arrangement is often called a pipeline because material progresses uniformly from one stage to the next. Example 2.2 illustrates the speedup possible from using a pipeline to perform instruction prefetching.

In reality, very few computations fit the pure pipeline model. For example, different automobiles may have different options. Only some automobiles are to have air conditioners installed—the air-conditioning instal-

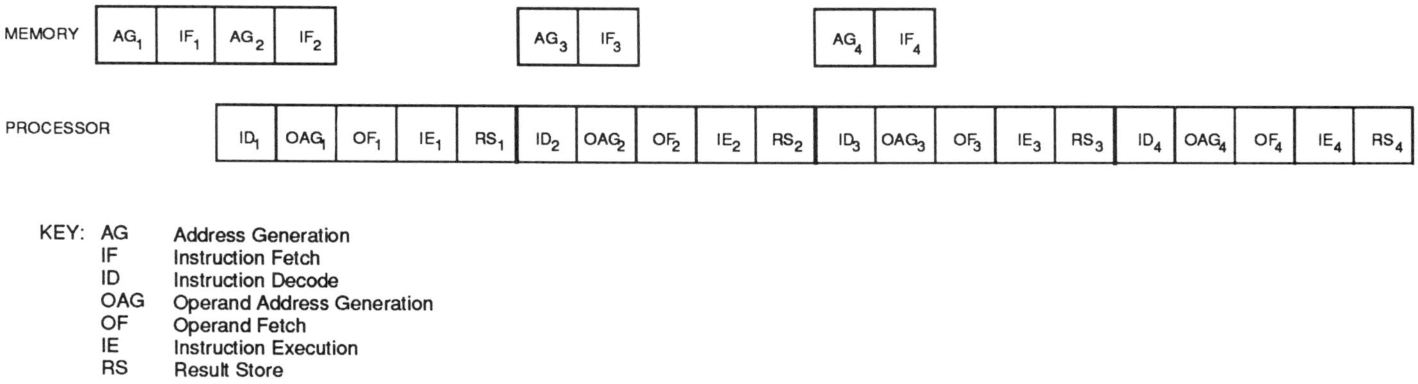

MEMORY

| | AG₁ | IF₁ | AG₂ | IF₂ | | | | AG₃ | IF₃ | | | | | AG₄ | IF₄ | | | | | |

PROCESSOR

| | | ID₁ | OAG₁ | OF₁ | IE₁ | RS₁ | ID₂ | OAG₂ | OF₂ | IE₂ | RS₂ | ID₃ | OAG₃ | OF₃ | IE₃ | RS₃ | ID₄ | OAG₄ | OF₄ | IE₄ | RS₄ |

KEY: AG   Address Generation
      IF   Instruction Fetch
      ID   Instruction Decode
      OAG Operand Address Generation
      OF   Operand Fetch
      IE   Instruction Execution
      RS   Result Store

FIGURE 2.12.   Timing of overlap between memory and processor.

45

EXAMPLE 2.2.   Instruction prefetch overlap.

The overlap created by the instruction prefetch effectively reduces the time to execute an instruction. Assume each phase of an instruction requires one unit of time, as illustrated in Figure 2.10. In a basic block containing N instructions, the first instruction requires seven units (instruction latency) and the $(N - 1)$ following instructions require five (the time for the processor to complete one operation—the "stage" time). The total time to complete the code segment is therefore

$$7 + (N - 1)5 = 2 + 5N$$

Compared with sequential execution, which takes $7N$ units for N instructions, the instruction prefetch buffer requires only

$$(5N + 2)/7N = 5/7 = 0.7$$

as much time for an apparent speedup of $7/5$ or 1.4. Note that each instruction still requires seven units of time to execute (the instruction latency), but an instruction is completed every five units of time (the instruction throughput).

lation stages will be idle a fraction of the time. If attempts are made to keep the air-conditioning stages fully occupied, there will be a problem merging the cars back into the rest of the assembly line. In a computer, a hardware multiplier that takes several clock cycles might cause a similar problem. Multiply instructions would either have to halt the pipeline while waiting for results or merge the results in to other computations in progress.

Exceptions and errors further complicate pipeline processing. For example, a new employee in charge of sealing the windshield may not be properly trained in the technique. The test for windshield sealing (i.e., showering the car with water) is typically several hours further down the assembly line. The defective procedure will have impacted several hundred cars before it is discovered. How should one fix this error? Should the assembly line be halted and the cars reinserted? Or should the cars be taken to the side and reworked? Exceptions in pipelines are perhaps one of the more difficult problems facing the computer designer.

A simple example of a pipeline exception is that of waiting for an operand to be fetched from memory. In simple integer units (including Titan's IPU), the entire CPU is halted while waiting for a cache miss to be serviced, because allowing other instructions to progress would introduce significant complexities into the hardware design.

Another problem is the interference that multiple pipelines might encounter when they utilize a single resource. For example, the instruction prefetch pipeline in Figure 2.12 depicts smooth operation between the memory and the processor. However, the processor also fetches operands from memory and stores results to memory. Conceptually, pipelines could be set up for operand fetching and storing. However, these operations would conflict with the instruction prefetch as they all use the single resource of the memory. An analogous situation in a car assembly line would be when a car needs two coats of different kinds of paint, making the painting robot a shared resource. This can be resolved by duplicating painting robots. (But what if the robots were so scarce that they couldn't be duplicated? Then there would be a scheduling problem.)

Single pipelines can have conflicts if not properly designed; however, these conflicts can be statically determined. It is usually not possible to model the interactions between multiple pipelines analytically. The computer designer frequently resorts to simulations in an attempt to identify situations when the pipelines conflict with each other. In fact, it is often possible to produce pipelines which maximally conflict with each other and contend for the same resource at every stage. Of course, this situation seldom arises in real machines, since designers are careful to avoid it.

2.4.3 BUS PROTOCOLS

In most contemporary systems, the available bus bandwidth limits the performance. Thus it is important to minimize the amount of nonproductive time on the bus. In addition, it is desirable to minimize the overhead of acquiring the bus in order to cut down the latency of retrieving information.

Bus protocols fall into two general categories: circuit-switched and message-switched. Figure 2.13 depicts a simplified protocol for each bus type. Most high-speed contemporary buses are synchronous (driven by a global clock) rather than asynchronous (driven by changing the state of bus control lines). Thus, the protocols in Figure 2.13 depict successive time "slots" on the bus.

Consider Figure 2.13a. Typically the requests and arbitration for the bus cycles occur concurrently with a current bus master using the address and data lines. In the case of no contention, a processor which desires to do a read-from-memory would request the bus. The bus arbiter (the logic that arbitrates requests for use of the bus among multiple simultaneous requestors) would grant the request; as soon as the bus was not busy, the processor would assert bus busy and place the address of the requested information on the address lines of the bus. In this example we are assuming it takes three bus slots for the memory to recognize its address, retrieve its data, and be ready to put it on the bus. When the data finally appears on the bus, the processor reads the data lines and deasserts the bus busy and

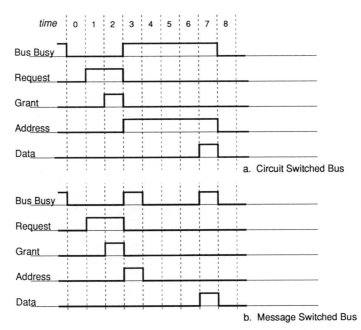

FIGURE 2.13.   Comparision of circuit- and message-switched bus protocols for a memory read operation.

address lines. For this transaction, the bus was busy for five slots—one slot to assert an address, three slots to access memory, and one slot to return data to the processor.

A message-switched bus (also called a disconnected bus, or split transaction bus, because the address and data portions of the bus cycle are not contiguous) is also shown in Figure 2.13b. In this case the processor relinquishes the bus as soon as it has presented the address. Other processors or I/O devices are now free to use the bus during the three time slots it takes for the data to be generated by the memory. When it is ready, the memory places the data on the bus and the memory read is completed. In this case, the bus is only occupied for two time slots—the address and data slots. Of course, the bus protocol has become more complex. For example, the processor has to provide extra information to the memory. In particular, it must identify itself so that when the memory retrieves the data it will arbitrate for the bus and assert the data as well as the identifier for the original requester so that the requester recognizes that the data is for it.

Titan uses a split-transaction, system-bus protocol to provide higher bus bandwidth. This allows Titan to initiate a new cycle on both the S-BUS and

R-BUS on every clock tick. As we shall see later, this results in approximately six times more available bus bandwidth than would be the case using a circuit-switched bus.

2.5 CONCURRENCY THROUGH REPLICATION

While concurrency through overlap is a powerful technique, it is eventually limited by the fact that the peak processing rate is achieved when all system resources are busy. The only way to improve performance beyond this point is to provide concurrency through replication of resources.

2.5.1 REPLICATION OF PROCESSORS

The simplest form of replication is to provide identical copies of resources that are explicitly controlled by the programmer. Figure 2.14 illustrates the addition of a second processor to our running example system. To see how additional processors might be used, consider the problem of multiplying each element of an array of numbers by a constant shown in Example 2.3.

Additional processors can effectively speed up programs in which the operations are completely independent of each other. However, most computations introduce data dependencies which must be preserved. Two such common dependencies are shown in Figure 2.17. In Figure 2.17a the second instruction utilizes the results of the computation of the first instruction. This is termed a Read After Write (RAW) hazard, in which the first instruction must be completed prior to the execution of the second

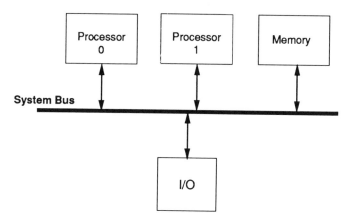

FIGURE 2.14. Simple example of parallelism through replication.

EXAMPLE 2.3.   Loop execution speedup.

Figure 2.15a illustrates a simple FORTRAN program to multiply the 100 elements of Array A by the constant 5. Because each computation inside the loop is independent of the other, a programmer could divide the problem between the two processors by having each processor execute the loop 50 times on different elements of the array as depicted in Figure 2.15b.

Typical assembly language for the do-loop in Figure 2.15a is depicted in Figure 2.16. There is an initialization phase where the count is established. Inside the loop for every element the address has to be calculated followed by the fetch, multiply, and store. The loop concludes with control opera-

```
        DO 10 I = 1,100
          A(I) = 5 * A(I)
     10 CONTINUE
```

a) Multiplication of a vector times a constant

Processor 0:

```
        DO 10 I = 1,50
          A(I) = 5 * A(I)
     10 CONTINUE
```

Processor 1:

```
        DO 20 J = 51,100
          A(J) = 5 * A(J)
     20 CONTINUE
```

b) The use of multiple processors to multiply a vector times a scalar

FIGURE 2.15.   Example of the use of replicated resources to speed up a computation.

```
        LOAD    COUNT,100        ! Set up
        LOAD    INDEX,0          ! Address calculation
  LOOP: LOAD    TEMP,A(INDEX)    ! Fetch
        MULT    TEMP,5           ! Multiply
        STORE   A(INDEX),TEMP    ! Store
        ADD     INDEX,DATASIZE
        DECR    COUNT            ! Loop control
        JNZ     LOOP
```

FIGURE 2.16.   Typical assembly language code for a "Do-Loop."

tions to determine whether the computation is finished. If each instruction requires seven phases (or clock "ticks") as assumed in Figure 2.10, then one iteration takes

$$(2 + 100 * 6 \text{ instructions}) * 7 \text{ ticks} = 4124$$

clock ticks to execute. The multiprocessor, on the other hand, would require

$$(2 + 50 * 6) * 7 = 2114$$

clock ticks for a speedup factor of 1.997. Linear speedup of 2 is not achieved because both processors must execute initialization instructions.

instruction. A method of synchronizing the execution of the instructions is required. An explicit mechanism such as the flag used in the producer/ consumer relationship buffers could be used.

An example of a Write After Read (WAR) hazard is shown in Figure 2.17b. In this case, we must ensure that the second instruction does not execute before the first instruction so that the value of Z is not changed before it is used to compute X. Figure 2.17c illustrates a Write After Write (WAW) hazard. We must ensure that the first instruction completes before the second instruction so that X contains the correct final value. Hazards can be prevented by the application programmer, automatically discovered and eliminated by compilers or detected at run-time in hardware and eliminated by stalling the dependent operation. Example 2.4 illustrates the impact of hazards on performance.

```
Y = memory(A)
X = Y + Z
```

(a) Example of a read-after-write (RAW) hazard.

```
X = Y + Z
Z = memory(A)
```

(b) Example of a write-after-read (WAR) hazard.

```
X = memory(A)
X = Y + Z
```

(c) Example of a write-after-write (WAW) hazard.

FIGURE 2.17.   Examples of data dependence.

EXAMPLE 2.4.   Hazards and their impact on speedup.

Consider the cosine function approximated by the first four terms of the Maclaurin series:

$$\cos(x) = 1 - x^2/(2!) + x^4/(4!) - x^6/(6!)$$
$$= 1 - x^2/2 + x^4/24 - x^6/720.$$

The MIPS R2000 with its five-stage pipeline would take 61 cycles to execute an iterative version of this expansion. One alternative is to unwind the loop as illustrated in Figure 2.18. To simplify the discussion on hazards we have assumed arithmetic instructions with three unique register operands. Consider a computer whose implementation of the instruction execute cycle has five stages: instruction fetch (F), instruction decode (D), execute (X), access memory (M), and write to registers (W). Assume all states take one clock tick except execution which is a function of the operation (Load = 1, ADD/SUB = 2, MULT/DIV = 4). Then the code in Figure 2.18 would take 81 clock ticks to execute. An idealized pipelined machine which ignored data hazards would take 18 clock ticks to execute this code as depicted in Figure 2.19. Note that due to differences in execution time, instructions can actually finish out of order. The idealized pipeline represents a speedup of a factor of 4.5 over the non-pipelined case.

Initial Conditions:

   x is in register F1.

   F0 is initialized to 0.

   The denominator coefficients (2, 24, and 720) are stored in array D.

   R4 contains the base address for array D.

Cosine Function:

01	MULTF	F2, F1, F1	! F2 = $x \cdot x$
02	LF	F3, 0(R4)	! F3 = D[1] = 2
03	DIVF	F4, F2, F3	! F4 = $x^2/2$
04	SUBF	F0, F0, F4	! F0 = $1 - x^2/2$
05	MULTF	F5, F2, F2	! F5 = x^4
06	LF	F6, 4(R4)	! F6 = D[2] = 24
07	DIVF	F7, F5, F6	! F7 = $x^4/24$
08	ADDF	F0, F0, F7	! F0 = $1 - x^2/2 + x^4/24$
09	MULTF	F8, F5, F2	! F8 = x^6
10	LF	F9, 8(R4)	! F9 = D[3] = 720
11	DIVF	F10, F8, F9	! F10 = $x^6/720$
12	SUBF	F0, F0, F10	! F0 = $1 - x^2/2 + x^4/24 - x^6/720$

FIGURE 2.18.   Code to calculate the first four terms of the Maclaurin series.

Instruction	1	2	3	4	5	6	7	8	9	10	11	12	13	14	15	16	17	18
MULTF	F	D	X	X	X	X	M	W										
LF		F	D	X	M	W												
DIVF			F	D	X	X	X	X	M	W								
SUBF				F	D	X	X	M	W									
MULTF					F	D	X	X	X	X	M	W						
LF						F	D	X	M	W								
DIVF							F	D	X	X	X	X	M	W				
ADDF								F	D	X	X	M	W					
MULTF									F	D	X	X	X	X	M	W		
LF										F	D	X	M	W	·			
DIVF											F	D	X	X	X	X	M	W
SUBF												F	D	X	X	M	W	

Cycle Number 1 2 3 4 5 6 7 8 9 10 11 12 13 14 15 16 17 18

FIGURE 2.19. Execution of the cosine program without hazards in a pipelined machine.

The idealized speedup is not obtainable due to hazards. Figure 2.20 depicts the hazards in the cosine code. Since some hazards span many instructions, they will not actually occur, since there will be sufficient time to complete execution of the first instruction prior to use of the data. Figure 2.21 illustrates the execution of the cosine code with the hazards accounted for by stalling subsequent instructions and by passing data directly from the write stage of one instruction to the execute stage of another. The pipeline now requires over twice as many cycles (38) to execute as the idealized pipeline (18) yielding a speedup of only 2.13 over the nonpipelined case.

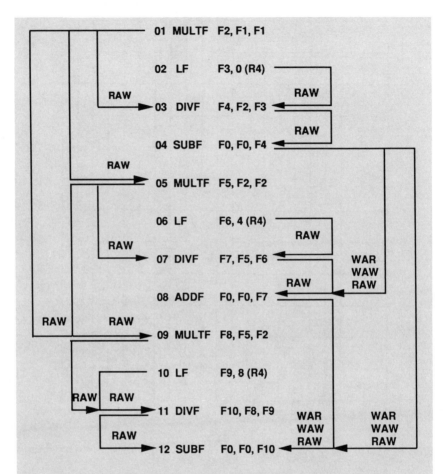

FIGURE 2.20.   Hazards in the Cosine Code.

FIGURE 2.21. Execution of the cosine code with the hazards avoided by stalling (denoted by a dash "—") and passing the results directly from a write stage to an execution stage (e.g., instruction 3 waiting for the results of instruction 1).

Instruction \ Cycle	1	2	3	4	5	6	7	8	9	10	11	12	13	14	15	16	17	18	19	20	21	22	23	24	25	26	27	28	29	30	31	32	33	34	35	36	37	38
MULTF	F	D	X	X	X	X	M	W																														
LF		F	D	X	M	W																																
DIVF			F	D	–	–	–	–	X	X	X	X	M	W																								
SUBF				F	D	–	–	–	X	X	M	W																										
MULTF					F	D	–	–	–	X	X	X	X	M	W																							
LF						F	D	–	–	–	X	M	W																									
DIVF							F	D	–	–	–	X	X	X	X	M	W																					
ADDF								F	D	–	–	–	X	X	M	W																						
MULTF									F	D	–	–	–	X	X	X	X	M	W																			
LF										F	D	–	–	–	X	M	W																					
DIVF																										F	D	–	–	–	X	X	X	X	M	W		
SUBF																											F	D	–	–	–	–	–	–	X	X	M	W

Cycle Number: 1 2 3 4 5 6 7 8 9 10 11 12 13 14 15 16 17 18 19 20 21 22 23 24 25 26 27 28 29 30 31 32 33 34 35 36 37 38

MULTF	F2, F1, F1	! F2 = $x \cdot x$
LF	F3, 0(R4)	! F3 = D[1] = 2
LF	F6, 4(R4)	! F6 = D[2] = 24
LF	F9, 8(R4)	! F9 = D[3] = 720
DIVF	F4, F2, F3	! F4 = $x^2/2$
MULTF	F5, F2, F2	! F5 = x^4
SUBF	F0, F0, F4	! F0 = $1 - x^2/2$
DIVF	F7, F5, F6	! F7 = $x^4/24$
MULTF	F8, F5, F2	! F8 = x^6
ADDF	F0, F0, F7	! F0 = $1 - x^2/2 + x^4/24$
DIVF	F10, F8, F9	! F10 = $x^6/720$
SUBF	F0, F0, F10	! F0 = $1 - x^2/2 + x^4/24 - x^6/720$

FIGURE 2.22. Rearrangement of the cosine code to minimize stalls due to hazards.

One way to avoid hazards is to have the compiler rearrange the code to move the hazards beyond the depth of the pipeline. If the cosine code is rearranged as in Figure 2.22, the code executes in 28 cycles, a speedup of 2.9 over the nonpipelined code.

As with the case of overlap, Titan uses replication in many areas to improve concurrency. Figure 2.23 highlights the replication:

- Multiple CPUs, each with an IPU and a VPU, may be used in a single Titan system.

- Multiple buses connect the memory with the rest of the system. The R and S buses provide high-speed data paths to the memory. The R-BUS is for reading only and provides blocks of data to the Vector Floating Point Unit (VPU). The S-BUS is the global store bus which can be used for both reads and writes.

- Separate pixel processors provide computation for each of the primary colors (red, green, and blue) and for Z buffering.

- The integer processing unit has separate buffers (caches) for data and instructions. Thus both an instruction and datum can be fetched in parallel.

- The vector register file is divided into four "banks," which are independently accessible. Thus data can be put into one bank while a second bank provides data to the Floating-Point Unit.

- Multiple memory controllers allow a block of consecutive memory words to be accessed concurrently.

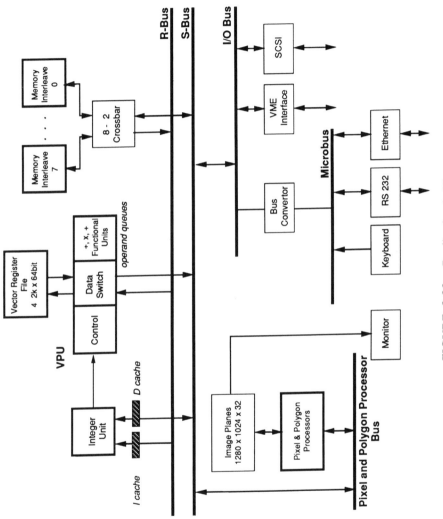

FIGURE 2.23. Replication in Titan.

57

2.5.2 REPLICATION OF CACHE MEMORIES

The Titan IPU, like many RISC processors, uses separate instruction-cache (I-cache) and data-cache (D-cache) memories. The advantage of using a split cache is that twice the memory bandwidth is available to the IPU because simultaneous memory accesses to instructions and data may be performed on the separate memories. This allows Titan to achieve the theoretical maximum of one instruction per clock cycle when both caches have a hit, even for load and store operations.

2.5.3 INTERLEAVED MEMORY

Another method of replication commonly used in high performance computer systems is interleaved memory. With interleaved memory, several different banks of memory each respond to different physical memory addresses to provide overlapped memory accesses by using multiple memory units.

Figure 2.24 depicts the typical timing of a memory controller. The memory controller observes that a read is requested and, after examining the address, determines that the desired data resides in its memory array. The memory controller accesses the memory array and produces the data. The time from the request to the availability of the data is called the access time (*t.access*). After an access the memory controller must reset itself and prepare for the next request. This time is called recovery (*t.recovery*). The combination of access and recovery time is called the memory cycle time (*t.cycle*).

The memory can respond to any number of requests provided that they do not arrive more frequently than once every memory cycle. The cycle

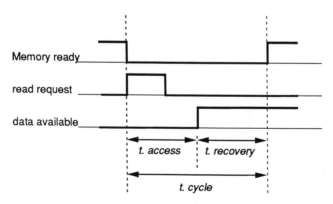

FIGURE 2.24. Typical memory operation.

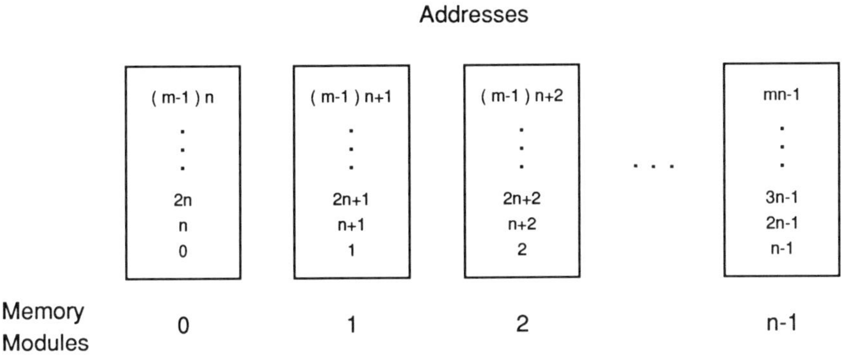

Addresses

FIGURE 2.25.   Assignment of $n \times m$ words to n memory modules.

time is approximately twice the access time for most contemporary memories. If references are spread among enough different memory modules, the apparent memory response time can come arbitrarily close to $t.access$. Each memory module will have an apparent response time of $t.access$ so long as it is not selected again within $t.recovery$. Thus, the $t.recovery$ is overlapped with requests to other memory modules.

A common way of staggering memory requests is to assign consecutive memory words to different memory controllers. Figure 2.25 illustrates low-order interleaving where consecutive words are stored in different memory modules. Figure 2.26 illustrates the timing for accessing five consecutive memory words with and without interleaving. In this diagram, it is assumed that the access time and recovery time are equal. Time to read N words without interleaving is $2N$. If we assume interleaving with two memory controllers (one for even addresses and one for odd addresses), the memory requests can only be issued every $t.access$ time. If a single bus is only able to request once per bus cycle (which is assumed to be equal to $t.access$ in this diagram), then the time to access N words is $(N + 1)$ $t.access$. The actual memory performance will be determined by the degree of interleaving, the ratio $t.cycle/t.access$, and the actual memory reference pattern. In the example of Figure 2.26 if only even address words were requested, the two-way interleaving would be no faster than the memory without interleaving.

If interleaving is extended to a large number of banks, the effect is to present a system memory which can respond to a memory access request in a time related to the access time of the memory chips used, completely hiding any recovery time. Furthermore, if many interleaves are used, system throughput can be increased by activating multiple interleaves in succession for successive memory access requests. Figure 2.27 shows that if

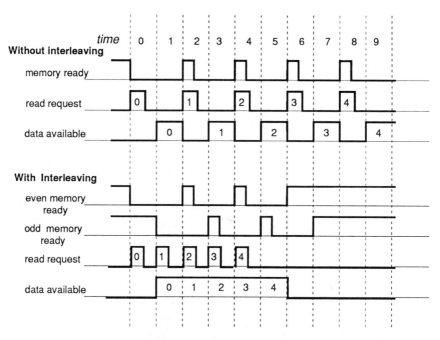

FIGURE 2.26.   Memory access times with and without two-way interleaving.

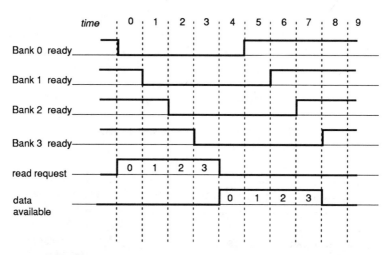

FIGURE 2.27.   Memory interleaving for increased memory bandwidth.

memory access time is five CPU cycles, activating four different memory interleaves (one on each cycle), can result in a total of four memory transfers in eight clock cycles.

Thus, we can see that providing a large number of interleaves not only increases available memory bandwidth by hiding the recovery time of the memory chips, but also allows multiple accesses to different memory interleaves to proceed in parallel.

2.5.4 REPLICATION AND SPECIALIZATION

There are cases when replicated units are functionally specialized for performance. The Titan system with a separated Integer-Processing Unit (IPU) and Vector Floating Point Unit (VPU) is an example. The IPU can be executing integer instructions or setting up a sequence of floating-point operations for the VPU while the VPU is performing a computation. Thus both integer and floating-point operations can be concurrently executed. Note, however, that the problem of chaining and hazards has to be solved in the case of dissimilar functional units, just as it had to be solved in the case of multiple identical units.

The Titan vector floating-point unit in turn has three functionally specialized arithmetic and logic units for addition, multiplication, and division. Chaining and hazard problems also must be resolved among the VPU functional units as well.

2.6   VECTOR OPERATIONS

By design, computers perform complex operations by executing a large number of primitive operations. Often these primitive operations are very repetitive in nature. Rather than processing a group of information element by element, the entire set of information can be treated as a single entity (sometimes called a block or a vector) and the instructions issued only once.

2.6.1 BLOCK-DATA TRANSFERS

Perhaps the simplest form of block or vector operation is the movement of data from one location to another. Historically, this was first introduced in input/output controllers. If a block of data (such as a page in a virtual memory system) had to be moved from input/output device into main memory, there was a substantial amount of overhead if the processor had to be interrupted to handle each data element individually. Thus, the concept of Direct Memory Access (DMA) evolved. Rather than have the processor request each data element individually (as it does when it accesses memory), the processor initializes the input/output controller with the beginning address of the location in memory where the data is to be stored and the number of data elements in the block. As the input/output controller fetches each data element, it requests the memory and stores the element at the designated address. Subsequently the address is incremented and the element count is decremented in preparation for storing the next data element as it is retrieved. The input/output controller proceeds until the entire block is transferred and only then interrupts the processor to notify it that the operation is completed.

Note that a block size of one is most effectively retrieved via a direct request (usually called a scalar operation). This direct request is a simple load or store instruction as seen on a conventional processor. When blocks are large, it is more effective to incur some startup overhead to set up a block operation (usually called a vector operation).

Since scalar operations have no overhead but vector operations move data at a faster average rate, there is typically a crossover point between individual and independent operations and block-oriented operations. The crossover point occurs when the vectors are long enough that the amortized overhead, when combined with the high speed of vector operations, is equal to the speed of a succession of scalar operations. Numbers for vector/scalar crossover points range from 10 to 100 vector elements on typical machines.

2.6.2   BLOCK ARITHMETIC OPERATIONS

The concept of vector operations can be carried beyond simple data transfers and extended to arithmetic operations. For example, consider multiplication of a vector times a constant as depicted by the do-loop in Figure 2.15. Typical scalar code for this loop was presented in Figure 2.16. To improve performance, we could define a new class of instruction that deals with vector rather than scalar values.

Consider the program in Figure 2.28. As with DMA there is a setup sequence to define the length and the starting address of the vector. The desired elements of the vector may not be physically adjacent in memory. For example, the matrix shown in Figure 2.29a is a two-dimensional array which must be converted into a single dimension for storage in memory. One way of storing the information is column by column (termed "column major form," the form used by the FORTRAN language) as depicted in Figure 2.29b. Now assume we want to access the first row of the matrix. First-row elements are stored at addresses 100, 103, 106, and 109. The elements we desire are stored a constant distance of three words apart.

Load	Length of A	! Setup for fetch
Load	Start address of A	
Load	Stride of A	
Load	Data size	
Load Vector	VR,A	! Fetch vector to VR
Load	Length of A	! Setup for multiply
Load	Data size	
Multiply	VR,5	! Multiply vector • scalar
Load	Length of A	! Setup for store
Load	Starting address of A	
Load	Stride of A	
Load	Data size	
Store Vector	A,VR	! Store result from VR

FIGURE 2.28.   Vector pseudocode for multiplying a vector by a scalar.

This distance is frequently referred to as the "stride" of the vector. Then we have to define the size of each of the individual elements in the vector. Vector elements could range from one to eight bytes in size.

Once the characteristics of the vector have been defined, the machine can execute instructions which manipulate the vector as a single entity. As in scalar machines, there are two basic approaches to manipulating vectors. First is a register-oriented organization where the data elements must be loaded into the registers prior to operation. This is the classic "load/store" architecture wherein the only memory operators are load and store and all arithmetic operations take place only on the contents of the registers.

The second approach is to define an instruction set which operates directly on memory. This eliminates the overhead of loading and storing the vector into a register file, but operation on each element of the vector now encounters the latency accessing the bus and subsequently the memory.

Of course, all the mechanisms which speed up memory accesses such as pipelining and buffering can be used to speed up access to the vectors. Note, however, that a single vector operation can easily saturate resources such as memory and bus bandwidth. Once a vector is resident in a cache, it requires no further memory/bus resources until it is either written out or replaced by some other data element. If the vector is larger than the buffer (e.g., the vector register file or the cache), performance will degrade as data is swapped in and out of the buffer. Typically, compilers attempt

$$\begin{vmatrix} a11 & a12 & a13 & a14 \\ \\ a21 & a22 & a23 & a24 \\ \\ a31 & a32 & a33 & a34 \end{vmatrix}$$

(a) A 3 x 4, two-dimensional matrix

address	element
100	a11
101	a21
102	a31
103	a12
104	a22
105	a32
106	a13
107	a23
108	a33
109	a14
110	a24
111	a34

(b) Storage of the two-dimensional matrix in column major form.

FIGURE 2.29.   The representation of a two-dimensional matrix in a one-dimensional array.

to identify vector operations and automatically split them up into smaller vectors if the vector size exceeds the capacity of the buffer.

2.6.3 OVERHEAD OF VECTOR OPERATIONS

Returning to Figure 2.28, we see three vector instructions—move the vector from memory to the vector registers (VR), multiply each element in the vector register by a constant five, and store the contents of the vector register. The controls for each vector instruction have to be set up prior to its execution. There are three sources of savings in Figure 2.28 over the code in Figure 2.16. The first is that there are no instructions to calculate the address of each element of the vector. Secondly, there are no instructions to test for the end of the vector (i.e., the end of the loop). Thirdly, the operation code for the vector instructions needs to be fetched only once, whereas the sequential machine must fetch the operation code for each instruction of every element in the vector. These savings are offset by the instructions required to set up each vector instruction.

Table 2.1 is a comparison of the number of cycles required to execute the multiplication of the vector times the scalar, assuming the loop is divided between various numbers of processors and vector units. Furthermore, all instructions are assumed to require the seven clock ticks depicted in Figure 2.10. The first column gives the organization while the second column gives the number of clock cycles for the operation in terms of the vector length N. The third column gives the relative time for the computation with infinitely long vectors compared with the uniprocessor case, while the fourth column gives a cycle count for the case of $N = 100$ elements.

The program in Figure 2.16 has three setup instructions plus six instructions in the loop which are each executed N times. The total number of cycles becomes seven times the total number of instructions. Dual and quad processors cut the loop size by a factor of 2 and 4 respectively, but both still need the three setup instructions.

The code in Figure 2.28 has 10 setup instructions at seven clock ticks each and three vector instructions. The vector instructions need to be fetched only once, using two clock cycles for address generation and instruction fetching. The remaining five phases of the instruction are assumed to execute each of the N elements in the vector. Again, multiple

TABLE 2.1. Comparison of the time required to execute the multiplication of a vector times a scalar for various organizations.

Organization	Cycles	Relative Time for Large N	Cycles for $N = 100$
Uniprocessor	$7(2 + 6N)$	1	4214
Dual Processor	$7(2 + 6N/2)$	0.500	2114
Quad Processor	$7(2 + 6N/4)$	0.250	1064
Single Vector Unit	$70 + 3(2 + 5N)$	0.357	1576
Dual Vector Unit	$70 + 3(2 + 5N/2)$	0.178	826
Quad Vector Unit	$70 + 3(2 + 5N/4)$	0.089	451
Pipelined Uniprocessor	$8 + 6N$	0.143	608
Pipelined Dual Processor	$8 + 6N/2$	0.071	308
Pipelined Quad Processor	$8 + 6N/4$	0.036	158
Pipelined Single Vector Unit	$16 + 3N$	0.071	316
Pipelined Dual Vector Unit	$16 + 3N/2$	0.036	166
Pipelined Quad Vector Unit	$16 + 3N/4$	0.018	91

vector units decrease the vector size accordingly. We see that for this problem a vector unit is 2.8 times faster than a uniprocessor. In addition, there are no data dependencies in the original loop, and the number of cycles required to execute the problem decreases almost linearly with the number of replicated processors or vector units. By setting the number of cycles required for the uniprocessor equal to those required for the single vector unit and solving for N, we can determine the crossover between the size of the vector and whether the scalar or vector unit is most advantageous. In this case we have

$$7(2 + 6N) = 70 + 3(2 + 5N)$$
$$27N = 62$$
$$N = 2.30.$$

The vector unit requires fewer clock ticks for vectors of length three or larger and is similar in the case for vectors of size two.

Of course, all the techniques we have described for speeding up a scalar instruction set can also be used on a vector instruction set. In particular, instructions could be pipelined. The bottom half of Table 2.1 illustrates the number of cycles required to complete the scalar and vector program, assuming every phase of each instruction is pipelinable.

In particular, the program in Figure 2.16 executes $6N + 2$ instructions and has a latency of six cycles to the completion of the first instruction. Multiple processors linearly reduce the number of cycles in a loop. The vector unit, on the other hand, has 10 scalar instructions plus a result every time-tick for the length of the vector (e.g., N) for each of the three vector instructions. There is also a latency of six prior to the availability of the result of the first instruction. Multiple vector units linearly decrease the size of the vector.

Figure 2.30 depicts the performance range covered by pipelined/non-pipelined and multiple processor/vector unit organizations. We see a range of speedup of over 50 to 1 for this particular problem for pipeline vector units. Of course, applications are more complicated than the simple loop. As we indicated, there are chaining and hazards which could prevent the pipeline from producing a result every cycle; furthermore, we were assuming that the multiple uses of shared resources (such as fetching instructions and data from the memory) did not interfere with each other.

There are techniques which can be used to speed up frequently encountered operations that do not apply uniformly to all computations. Some of these techniques include the following:

Multiple data paths for providing concurrency.   For example, the floating-point unit might have DMA logic for simultaneously loading two

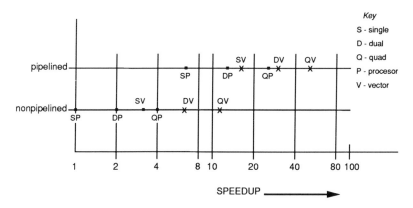

FIGURE 2.30. Relative performance of pipelined and nonpipelined versions of multiplication of a vector times a scalar.

different vectors. Thus the typical binary operation between two vectors requires only one vector load-time, not two.

Special by-pass data paths. If the results of one computation are used directly in a second computation, the data from the first computation can be fed directly to the arithmetic logic units rather than being stored and subsequently retrieved.

Special instructions to minimize vector setup overhead. For example, if the length of vector **A** in Figure 2.28 remains the same for all three vector operations, the hardware could remember the vector length between instructions, saving a separate load. The same could be done for all vector characteristics. It may be possible to store multiple vector characteristics in a single instruction. Indeed, certain instructions could be defined to have default values for vector characteristics (such as unit stride and four-byte data size) that become defaults when the vector starting address is loaded.

2.6.4 CONTEXT SWITCHING COSTS

All contemporary large computer operating systems allow multiple programs to coexist in memory and provide mechanisms for switching execution between them. A very simple example is a main computational process and an input/output process. The processor executes the computational problem until the input/output device indicates via an interrupt that it requires some attention. The operating system will switch execution to the input/output program and upon completion will return control to the computational program.

The partial state of a process must be stored away when it is swapped out so that it can be restored and processing can be resumed when it is next allowed to execute. The size of this context-switching state affects the cost of saving state, which adds directly to the latency and consequently the overhead of initiating processes. The various buffers in a machine are part of this process state. In the case of a cache, the contents of modified locations might have to be written back to memory (depending on whether a write-through or copy-back strategy is used), and information for the new process would have to be read in. This context change takes place automatically in a demand-driven fashion over a period of time after the context switch as cache accesses are made by the new process, but none-theless, the cost can be considerable. The vector registers, on the other hand, are software-controlled buffers. If multiple register files are pro-vided, the registers need not be saved on a context swap—only the pointer to the register file needs to be changed.

2.7   LIMITS TO SPEEDUP: AMDAHL'S LAW

With the large variety of speedup techniques just described, one might think that any program can be sped up by an arbitrary amount simply by adding enough pipeline stages and parallel processors. Unfortunately, life in the supercomputer world seldom works out that way. The reason is that most programs have only a limited amount of code that may be parallelized or vectorized. Thus, the speedup techniques apply only to a portion of the program.

Amdahl's Law (Amdahl, 1967) states that the performance improvement to be gained from using some speedup in execution is limited by the frac-tion of the code on which the speedup technique can be used. In other words, speeding up only a portion of a program brings diminishing returns as that one portion of a program gets faster and faster. This phenomenon occurs because as one portion of a program becomes increasingly faster, it accounts for a decreasing portion of total execution time, limiting poten-tial further gains. In the limiting case, if a portion of a program were made infinitely fast, the rest of the program would still take some finite amount of time.

The amount of speedup possible is limited to the portion of time taken up by the code the speedup technique is applied to in the original pro-gram. For example, if one-half the code can be parallelized, then the pro-gram can not be made more than twice as fast using even an infinite amount of parallelization, since the original one-half of the code that can-not be parallelized must still execute. Example 2.5 shows a more detailed explanation of this effect.

EXAMPLE 2.5. An example of Amdahl's Law.

Let us examine the effect of Amdahl's Law on a parallel processing environment. Assume that the following code is to be sped up using parallel processing:

```
. . . . computation of B(J) and C(J) . . . .

              A = B(J) * C(J)
              DO 100 I = 1,10000
                 X(I) = Y(I) * A
        100 CONTINUE
```

Let us assume that the computation of A takes 100 times longer than the computation of $X(I)$, and that there is zero cost incurred for looping overhead. Then, the computation of A is non-parallelizable and costs 100 units while the computation of X may be parallelized using up to 10,000 processors. The total computation time is 10,100 units.

The table below shows the total execution time for the computation with varying numbers of processors:

# Processors	A	$X(I)$	Total	Speedup
1	100	10,000	10,100	1.00
10	100	1,000	1,100	9.18
100	100	100	200	50.50
1,000	100	10	110	91.82
10,000	100	1	101	100.00

From this data, we see that as the first 10 processors are added, nearly linear speedup is obtained. As we add more processors, the relative execution time for $X(I)$ becomes smaller and smaller with respect to the execution time for A. At 1000 processors, $X(I)$ takes only 10% as long as A to compute, so adding another 9000 processors results in only a 10% speed improvement.

From this example, it seems that the diminishing returns start to become noticeable at about when the computation of A and $X(I)$ take the same amount of time. A good architectural rule of thumb is to concentrate on speeding up the portion of the computation that takes the longest amount of time in order to get the best effect for resources spent.

More formally, Amdahl's Law can be stated mathematically. If t_s is the execution time, assuming the programs were executed sequentially, and t_p

the time, assuming parallel exectution, then the potential speedup is

$$S = t_s/t_p.$$

However, if only the fraction f of a program can be executed in parallel, the execution time is

$$t_f = (1 - f)t_s + ft_p$$

yielding a speedup of

$$t_s/t_f = \frac{1}{(1 - f) + f/S}.$$

Amdahl's Law applies to a surprisingly large number of aspects of computer operations. Specific areas include the following:

Vectorization.   Vector units speed up many loops and array accesses but do not help with control logic and scalar operations.

Parallelization.   Many portions of code are not inherently parallel. Non-parallelized code can either be executed on a single processor or replicated among processors. In either case, sequential code limits potential speedup.

Replication of resources.   Functional units that are replicated cannot be used simultaneously in all portions of a program, limiting available speedup.

Addition of a pipeline.   Operations such as conditional branches force bubbles or delays in pipelines that prevent attaining the full potential speedup available.

Addition of cache memory.   Any hit ratio of less than 100% incurs large penalties for main memory access, which can quickly lengthen program execution time.

Whenever fast hardware support is provided for a specialized mode of operation (notably multiple CPUs and vector units), it is inevitable that a significant portion of time will be spent in nonspecialized modes of operation. We shall not consider Amdahl's Law in our further analysis, since its effects depend on the software's being executed and not the hardware; however, whenever we state that there will be some overhead time during which vector units or extra CPUs will be idle in subsequent discussions, we do so with the assurance that any real application program will behave in accordance with Amdahl's Law.

TABLE 2.2.   The relative order in which techniques are typically added to increase performance. Cost and performance increase as a function of distance from the top of the table.

Scaler	Vector
Registers	
Instruction Prefetch	
Write Buffer	
Bus Protocol + Block Transfer	
Cache	Register/Cache + Block Transfer
Pipelining	Pipelining
Memory Interleaving	
Parallel Processor	Bus Protocol + Memory Interleaving
	Parallel Processor

2.8   Summary

Each architecture and its implementation is a unique combination of the techniques discussed in this chapter. In general it is not possible to give an absolute ordering for adding performance enhancement features to a design; however, a partial ordering can be suggested. Table 2.2 depicts a rough ordering of the techniques with cost and performance increasing the further down the table we proceed. The first major decision is which data types will be supported. The decision to include vectors implies a minimal amount of investment to derive an advantage from the increment. While most decisions on what techniques to include can be made relatively independently, some techniques must be designed concurrently. For example, the decision to include memory interleaving implies that the bus protocol supports multiple accesses to sequential memory locations. Consider all techniques simultaneously in order to arrive at an effective design, otherwise, the system will be unbalanced and have its performance limited by one or more bottlenecks. An effective architecture is a puzzle in which all the pieces mesh and the components reach saturation at the same time.

Selection of the various speedup techniques and determining how they mesh with each other are the major tasks for the chief architect. You will see how all these various techniques interact during the detailed discussion of the Titan architecture in Chapter 5. Before we explore Chapter 5, however, we must discuss how architectural alternatives are evaluated. In particular, the concept of performance balance in an architecture is introduced in Chapter 3, and a model for understanding the components of execution costs is introduced in Chapter 4.

CHAPTER
THREE

PERFORMANCE
AND
BALANCE

Performance is measured in operations per unit of time or, conversely, the time needed to complete a specific operation. The concept of performance exists throughout the digital design hierarchy. Table 3.1 shows that at the semiconductor physics level, for example, the time to drain the charge at a PN junction would relate to the transistor turnoff time at the circuit level, which, in turn, would determine gate propagation delay at the switching circuit level. Gate delays, along with the topological interconnection of the gates both at the chip and printed circuit-board level, determine the time to execute a register–transfer operation. The sequence of register transfers, along with their execution times, determines the time required to execute an instruction. Finally, the system performance is determined by the mix of instructions required for a particular application.

There are at least two types of performance measures: probabilistic and deterministic. Probabilistic measures take into account statistical variations in the manufacturing process (e.g., transistors will actually have a range of turnoff times), the system design (e.g., hardware and software), and activity within the system (e.g., gate propagation delay varies as a function of the number and states of other gates driven, and the states of these other gates vary with their inputs). Deterministic measures attempt to remove the variations by assuming worst-case, average-case, or weighted-average statistics.

For the purposes of this discussion, statistical variations in the first four

TABLE 3.1.   Performance examples.

Typical Level	Performance Measure	Factors at This Level Affecting Performance
Semiconductor physics	Time to drain charge from PN junction	Junction dimensions Doping concentration Doping profile
Circuit	Transistor turnoff time	Transistor gain Operating point of transistor as determined by its interconnection with other circuit elements (e.g., resistors or voltage supplies) Stray capacitance, inductance
Gate	Gate propagation delay	Gate fan-in/fan-out
Register-transfer	Time to perform a register transfer	Data-path configuration (e.g., number of gates in data path) Control organization
Instruction set architecture	Time to perform an instruction	Sequence of register-transfer operations
System	Time to perform an application	Instruction mix in application System software System configuration Variations in input to the application

levels (i.e., semiconductor physics, circuit, gate, and register–transfer) will be ignored. These variations normally stem from the processes of design and manufacturing (e.g., transistors on different semiconductor chips will have slightly different characteristics). Since the hardware must work under all conditions, and since most newer systems have few asynchronous components, conservative worst-case design practices combined with fixed-frequency clocks usually eliminate these statistical variations.

TABLE 3.2.   Various performance measures as a function of level.

Level	Deterministic Measures	Probabilistic Measures
Hardware	Single parameters Typical instruction time Memory size Multiple parameters Kiviat graph	Average instruction execution time Information rate Weighted average instruction execution time
Instruction set architecture	Latency of various operations	Benchmarks
System	Instruction mixes Processor model	Synthetic benchmarks Queuing models

One of the primary uses of performance measures is in the comparison of systems. The performance measure selected then depends on the level of comparison to be used. Table 3.2 illustrates some of these levels and some of the measures to be discussed in the following subsections.

3.1 HARDWARE PERFORMANCE MEASURES

Because they directly reflect the state of technology, hardware performance measures are the easiest to determine or derive. They can be used to determine whether increased performance (e.g., transfer rate from a disk) can be absorbed in an existing system or what the most cost-effective component might be.

Occasionally hardware performance parameters are used to predict systems performance. Frequently manufacturers will list a series of deterministic parameters to give a "feel" for the system performance. Such a list might include:

- Time to execute a register–register ADD instruction,
- Average number of clock ticks to execute an instruction,
- Instruction-set size,
- Primary memory access time, cycle time, size,
- Cache access time, cycle time, size, and
- Secondary memory access time, transfer rate, and size.

Figure 3.1 expands the simple processor/memory/input/output diagram of the basic uniprocessor given in Chapter 2. It lists a set of six primary parameters that could be used to specify system performance. The PMS (Processor, Memory, Switch) notation is used in this chapter (Siewiorek et al., 1982).

There are seven primitives in PMS: processor P which interprets programs; memory M which holds information; data unit D which combines and changes the meaning of information; link L which transfers information from one place to another; switch S which constructs a link between other components; transducer T which changes the form of information (e.g., from magnetic domains to charge); and controller K that evokes operations in other components. The main components can be modified by attribute. Common attributes are p for primary as in Mp, s for secondary as in Ms, and c for central as in Pc.

3.1.1 Pc

Perhaps the single most important parameter is the performance of the processor. Historically, processor performance has been measured in

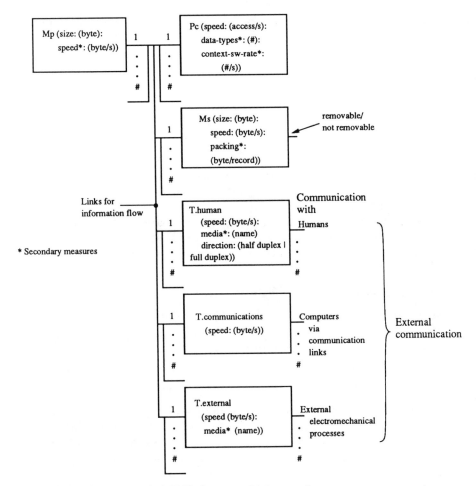

FIGURE 3.1. A typical PMS diagram with key performance parameters given.

instructions per second (*ips*). The number of instructions per second can be estimated by using the time of a single representative instruction or by the average instruction execution time (assuming all instructions are equally likely). A more accurate measure is a weighted average of instruction execution time using weights derived from a general instruction mix or from the intended application. Note that the instruction order of execution is very important in vector machines.

However, because of variations in instruction semantics, the *ips* measure is not always accurate. For vector/array machines which operate on multiple elements per single instruction, instructions per second would be a poor measure. As an extreme example, hand-held calculators have high-level, complex instructions, such as the sine function and polar-to-Cartesian coordinate conversion. In this case using anything but a final benchmark program would be misleading.

3.1.1.1 MEMORY ACCESSES PER SECOND

An alternate Pc performance measure is memory accesses per second. This is somewhat better because a single vector instruction may touch dozens or hundreds of data elements. Even though accesses per second is used as the Pc measure in this chapter, the reader should be aware that there is no single measure that is accurate independent of instruction set. Consider the case of Reduced Instruction-Set Computers (RISCs) and Complex Instruction-Set Computers (CISCs). The simpler RISC instructions execute faster but may require as much as twice the number of instructions to do the same amount of work as a CISC. Since RISCs are load/store architectures (i.e., load data into registers, manipulate, and store back into memory upon completion), the number of memory accesses per instruction is typically less than half that of the CISC (i.e., manipulate data directly in memory). Since instruction behavior is predictable, instructions cache more effectively than data, potentially leading to a reduced memory access rate after the cache for the same amount of work.

Another metric that is often proposed is the average number of Clocks Per Instruction (CPI) required. CPI typically favors RISC computers, since the simpler instruction can execute with fewer hazards. But pipelining techniques used on CISCs are closing the CPI gap.

3.1.1.2 VECTOR PERFORMANCE MEASURES

Because vector machines tend to have designs that are different from and more specialized than general purpose uniprocessors, they have come to be measured by some of their own special criteria. Typical metrics quoted for vector machines include peak vector rate, vector start-up time, instruction latency, vector/scalar break-even point, maximum achievable performance, vector load latency, and vector length at which one-half the maximum performance is achieved.

The numbers for these vector metrics will vary on different operations even in the same machine. For example, the rates are usually higher and the latency lower for addition than division. Typical single-vector operations such as a scalar times a vector, a vector times a vector, a scalar times a vector added to a vector, or an arbitrary binary vector operation with the vectors in memory are sometimes used as simple benchmarks.

The peak vector rate is sometimes estimated by adding up the data processing rates of all the functional units. In practice, this rate will never be achieved because computations will not require all functional units and data paths are usually insufficient to keep all functional units supplied with data. Since the bus between processor and memory is usually the limiting factor, a more meaningful metric might be the number of floating-point numbers supplied per second.

For example, consider a single binary floating-point operation where the data is not reused. There are two operands and one result. If each floating-point number is double precision (i.e., 64 bits) then each floating-point operation requires 24 bytes. An estimate of the number of double precision floating-point operations per second that an architecture can sustain would be the bus bandwidth divided by 24. Example 3.1 shows a performance estimate based on bus bandwidth for Titan.

In vector machines there is often a peak performance and an average performance. The peak performance, sometimes called the "guaranteed-not-to-exceed performance," is the upper limit possible in the situation where all data to be operated on is immediately available with no waiting and all floating-point computation units (typically both the multiplier and the floating-point adder) are in use simultaneously. The average performance, which is usually a more representative number of the capabilities of the machine, is the performance measured on some real application program or sequence of frequently occurring operations.

Two quantities that may be used to give a feel for the performance of a vector machine independent of specific programs are r^∞ and $n^{1/2}$. r^∞ is the maximum possible instruction execution rate for an infinite length vector.

EXAMPLE 3.1.   Bus bandwidth as an estimate of performance.

In Titan, the R-BUS that connects the memory to the floating-point unit has a bandwidth of 128 Mbytes per second. When performing matrix reduction operations, three inputs are required for every two operations (a multiplication and an addition per three inputs). Since each input is eight bytes in size, this gives:

$$\frac{16 \text{ M inputs}}{\text{sec}} * \frac{2 \text{ operations}}{3 \text{ inputs}} = 10.66 \text{ MFLOPS}$$

On the standard LINPACK benchmark, Titan achieves 10.5 MFLOPS with one processor for large input array sizes, confirming the calculation (and showing that Titan is very efficient at using its available resources in actual programs).

This number amortizes the costs associated with starting a vector over an infinite number of vector elements, making those costs negligible.

The r^∞ value for a processor is calculated by taking the number of cycles required to do a kernel operation such as those mentioned above (i.e., scalar times a vector, vector times a vector, scalar times a vector added to a vector, and a binary operation of two operands) as a function of N, the length of the vector. This number of cycles is then divided by M, the number of operations, and the limit taken as N goes to infinity. This yields the number of cycles for each result. The number of MFLOPS is then the system clock frequency divided by the number of clocks per result. Section 2.6.3 gives an example of how such a calculation is performed.

Another measure of the efficiency of the vector architecture is the vector length at which one-half the maximum achievable performance is reached; $n^{1/2}$ is the length of a vector (number of elements in the vector) that achieves one-half the r^∞ computation rate. The lower the $n^{1/2}$, the better the performance on short vectors and on real programs in general. The longer the required vector length, the more overhead and more inefficient the vector architecture. Example 3.2 calculates these parameters for the scalar times vector example worked out in Example 2.1.

3.1.1.3 SECONDARY Pc PARAMETERS

The secondary Pc parameters include the number of data types and the context-switching rate. The number of data types (e.g., integer, scalar, real,

---

EXAMPLE 3.2. Two typical operation metrics for a vector machine.

Maximum Achievable Performance (r^∞):
Pipelined uniprocessor cycles for scalar $*$ vector $= 8 + 6N$

$$\lim_{n \Rightarrow \infty} \frac{\text{Cycles/operation}}{\text{number of operations}} = \lim_{n \Rightarrow \infty} \frac{(8 + 6N)}{N}$$
$$= 6 \text{ cycles for each result}$$

If cycles/second $= 16$ million

$$\text{Then } r^\infty = \frac{16 \text{ M cycles/sec}}{6 \text{ cycles/op}} = 2.67 \text{ MFLOPS}$$

Vector length at which one-half r^∞ is obtained ($n^{1/2}$):

$$\frac{8 + 6N}{N} = 2 * 6$$
$$n^{1/2} = N = 1.33$$

string, character, list, vector) in the Pc gives an indication of performance when it is operated with a particular language. In the case of multiprogramming systems (e.g., real time control, transaction processing, and time sharing), the time to switch from job to job is critical. Thus, the process context-switching rate is also an important attribute, because most large computer systems operate with some form of multiprogramming.

Bus bandwidth is an important issue for balance within the system. It is not directly observable to the outside world in the same manner as other measures but is nonetheless an important metric of balance. In fact, memory bandwidth can be used as a predictor of performance for some applications. (Miranker *et al.*, 1989)

3.1.2   Mp, Ms

The memory sizes (in bytes) for both primary and secondary memory give a measure of memory capability. The memory transfer rates are needed as secondary measures, especially to compute memory interference when multiple processors are used. The Mp transfer rate also tracks the access rate available in the Pc for secondary memory transfers and external interface transfer.

File systems may require multiple accesses to directories, even when reading only a single item of data; therefore, file system activity depends strongly on file organization as well as data-access patterns, and a probabilistic measure of file access rate is needed for a more accurate performance estimate. Similarly, for multiprogrammed systems, which use secondary memory to hold programs, the probabilistic measure of program swapping rate is required.

3.1.3   T.human, T.communications, T.external

Communications capabilities with humans, other computers and other electronically encoded processes are equally important performance attributes. Each interconnection (usually called a channel) has a certain data rate and direction (half-duplex for two-way communication but in only one direction at a time, full-duplex for simultaneous two-way communication).

Collectively, the data rates and the number of channels connected to each of the three different environments (people, computers, other electronically encoded processes), signify quite different styles of computing capability, structure, and function. For example, the absence of any communications connection to other computers implies a stand-alone system. Interconnection only to mechanical processes via electronically encoded links implies a real time structure. Similarly, human intercommunication with multiple terminals denotes a time-sharing or transaction-processing orientation.

On Titan, communication via graphics is an important performance attribute. Two important numbers for measuring this communication bandwidth are the speed of drawing lines and the speed of drawing triangles. Line-drawing speed is usually given in the form "vectors per second," which refers to the number of line segments of a relatively short length (say 10 to 50 pixels), which may be drawn per second. Triangle-drawing speed is likewise given for an arbitrarily defined triangle size (say 100 pixels) in terms of the number of triangles per second.

3.2 KIVIAT GRAPHS

It is often convenient to summarize the various performance metrics graphically. This not only gives a concise representation of the various performance parameters, but can also provide a visual clue as to the balance of the system.

Figure 3.2 uses a Kiviat graph to display the six main performance dimensions—processing, primary and secondary memory capacity, and the three communication channels—in a single six-dimensional graph, with three secondary dimensions.

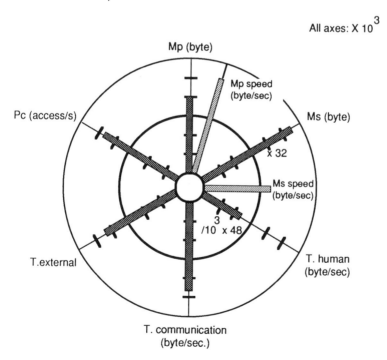

FIGURE 3.2.   Kiviat graph for the Cray 1.

Each dimension is shown on a logarithmic scale up to a factor of one million, with the value one denoting the absence of an attribute (e.g., where there is no communication with external systems beyond human interaction). Various secondary measures are also represented.

In the case that a dimension takes on values greater than one million, all axes are multiplied by a scale factor such that the largest value will fit. The scale factor, if other than one, is noted at the top of each Kiviat graph. For example, the outer ring in Figure 3.2 represents one billion (10^9) after scaling. When a scale factor is used, the value for some dimensions (e.g., communications with humans) may not be large enough to plot. Rather than erroneously indicate the absence of a dimension, the global scale factor is negated by dividing by a local scale factor denoted by the divide sign (/). All values are for the aggregated system. For example, the Ms dimension represents the total number of bytes on secondary storage (usually assumed to be disk unless otherwise noted).

Kiviat graphs were first used to summarize workload-specific performance with dimensions such as Pc, Ms, Pio busy, and the relative amount of time the Pc or Ms or Pio is the only active subsystem (Ferrari, 1978). The Kiviat graph concept has been adopted and modified as a means for summarizing hardware performance (Siewiorek *et al.*, 1982).

Parameters of individual components can be plotted with a multiplication factor (denoted by *x*) indicating the number of identical components in the system. Multiplication factors, usually found on the Ms and T.human dimensions, are applied when there is one dominant component type dictating the value of a dimension. Occasionally dimensions are further specified (e.g., audio, video). The graph conventions include subtleties of showing fixed points (i.e., ROM or hardwired), averages, and range. The arrangement of the six dimensions allows easy recognition of a structure in terms of the relative mix of the resource and performance attributes. Figure 3.3 gives a diagram of a computer system in the same order as the graph's dimensions.

The architects of the IBM System/360 postulated two rules of thumb for a balanced system. The first, Case's ratio, related Pc speed with Mp size, stating that 1 byte of Mp was required to support each instruction per second (ips). The second, Amdahl's rule (not to be confused with Amdahl's Law from Chapter 2), related Pc speed with I/O bandwidth, stating that one bit of I/O was required to support each instruction per second. Note that if the Pc speed is "balanced" with Mp size according to Case's ratio (1 byte of Mp per ips), then the value of the two dimensions should be about the same. These rules of thumb were postulated over 25 years ago when the dominant mode of computation was batch. To satisfy the demands of a contemporary multiprocessing environment, the amount of memory and I/O should be multiplied by approximately a factor of eight.

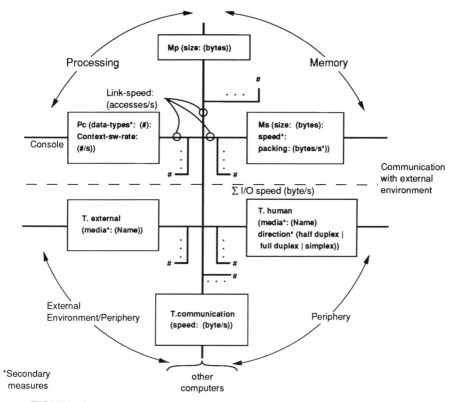

FIGURE 3.3. Rearrangement of the PMS diagram given in Figure 3.2.

Thus, the Kiviat graph not only summarizes major performance parameters but also graphically depicts the balance of a system. The relative capacity of processor, memory, and I/O is immediately discernible from the Kiviat graphs.

Figure 3.2 shows the Kiviat graph for a Cray computer, which is typical of a high-performance supercomputer. Figure 3.4 shows the Kiviat graph for a Titan computer. Note that the balance of the system is similar, but with Titan having better T.human capacity because of its graphics capabilities.

3.3   SYSTEM PERFORMANCE MEASURES

In order to measure the performance of a specific computer (e.g., a VAX) it is necessary to know the instruction set, the hardware performance, and the frequency of use for the various instructions. If the vector **U** is the

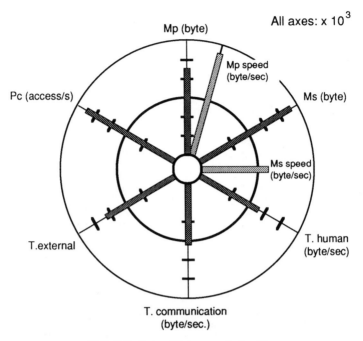

FIGURE 3.4.   Kiviat graph for Titan.

fractional utilization of each instruction and the vector **T** is the time to execute each instruction, then the execution time **E** is the dot product of **U** and **T**.

There are three ways to estimate the instruction utilization **U** and hence obtain **T**: each provides increasingly better answers. The first way is to arbitrarily select some instruction such as register-to-register addition as being a typical or average instruction, assign it a utilization of 100%, and simply use its execution time as the average execution time.

The second way to estimate instruction utilization is to use "standard" benchmarks to characterize precisely a machine's performance. The frequency of execution of instructions in the benchmark can be measured to give the value for each U_i. The execution times T_i can be estimated from the processor's instruction-set documentation. In general, this is a difficult task, since the execution time of individual instructions can vary widely depending on whether it is in cache, the architecture supports multiple function units and out-of-order instruction execution, etc. The execution time for an instruction is not a constant but rather a function of what other instructions precede and follow it. An attempt to calibrate the calculated execution time is to compare the actual running time of the benchmark to the calculated result **E** if the total number of instructions executed by the benchmark is known. Unfortunately, the accuracy of this measure for comparing architectures depends on the degree to which the selected benchmark reflects actual use of the system.

The third way to estimate instruction utilization would be the use of a specific, unique program when the actual use has not been characterized in terms of the standard benchmark (and may even not be easily characterized in terms of any specific benchmark, either). In this case it may be that no attempt is made to actually measure instruction utilization, but rather a final elapsed wall-clock time figure is used as a performance measurement. Use of this last alternative is warranted for real time and transaction processing, where computer selection and installation are predicated on running exactly one set of programs as efficiently as possible.

3.3.1   TYPICAL INSTRUCTIONS

The simplest single parameter of performance—instruction time for a simple operation (e.g., ADD)—was used in the first two computer generations, especially since high-level languages were less frequently used. Such a metric is an approximation of the average instruction time. It assumes (1) that all machines have about the same instruction set and that there is little difference among instructions within each instruction set; (2) that a specific data type such as single precision integer will be used much more heavily than others; and (3) that a typical add time will be given (e.g., the operand is in a random location in main memory rather than being cached or in a fast register).

It is possible to determine the average instruction time by executing one of every possible instruction. However, since the instruction use depends so much on which programs are executed, this metric is poor. A better measure is to keep statistics about the use of all programs and to give the average instruction time based on use of all programs. The usefulness of such a measure is for the comparison of two different implementations of the same architecture. It is inadequate when applied to measure a specific implementation or to compare two completely different architectures.

3.3.2   TYPICAL INSTRUCTION MODELS

It is possible to predict performance on the basis of a small number of fundamental deterministic measures. Such a model is illustrated in Table 3.3. The performance equation contains terms for both the processor and memory. Each parameter is affected by various implementation techniques as well as by basic technology.

Table 3.4 depicts the features used in Titan to affect each of the four

TABLE 3.3.   A simple model of processor performance.

$$\frac{1}{\text{performance}} = \underbrace{K1 \, t1}_{\substack{\text{processor} \\ \text{logic}}} + \underbrace{K2 \, t2}_{\substack{\text{memory} \\ \text{read pause}}}$$

Number of microcycles[1] per machine instruction:

$K1$ (microcycles/operation)

Ways to decrease $K1$:
  Multiple registers or register sets
  Multiple data paths
  Multiple functional units
  Processor/memory overlap
  Fewer microsteps (simpler decoding, more parallelism, etc.)
  Multiplexing processor logic (e.g., CDC 6600 barrel)
  More efficient instruction set
  Tailor microstep flow according to macro-instruction usage frequency

Data-path cycle time: $t1$ (seconds/microcycle)

Ways to decrease $t1$:
  Faster technology (e.g., for whole data path or only critical components)
  Shorter microcycles (e.g., multiple-length microcycles)
  Shorter physical data paths
  More efficient microinstruction fetch (microcoded machines only) (e.g., interleaved con-
    trol stores, multiple microword fetch, pipeline microword fetch/execution)
  Simple instruction formats to decrease decoding and control logic

Memory used per operation: $K2$ (bits/operation)

Ways to decrease $K2$:
  Increase operand bits/instruction (e.g., scalar vs serial data types, vector vs scalar data
    types)
  More efficient instruction set

Memory access time: $t2$ (seconds/bit)

Ways to decrease $t2$:
  Faster technology
  Apparent speedup (e.g., I/O spaces, caches)
  Widening word access (e.g., making data path wider, multiple fetches on a multiplexed
    bus)
  More efficient utilization of bandwidth (e.g., instruction prefetch, processor/memory
    overlap)

[1] In some machines "clock" or "clock tick" is used instead of the word microcycle.

TABLE 3.4. Titan features affecting the performance model.

$$\frac{1}{\text{performance}} = \underbrace{K1\ t1}_{\substack{\text{processor} \\ \text{logic}}} + \underbrace{K2\ t2}_{\substack{\text{memory} \\ \text{read pause}}}$$

Number of microcycles per machine instruction:

$K1$ (microcycles/operation)

Ways used to decrease $K1$:
- Multiple registers or register sets—vector registers
- Multiple data paths—vector load pipes
- Multiple functional units—(IPU, VPU) $\times$ 4, parallel processing
- Processor/memory overlap—cache, prefetch, pipelining
- More efficient instruction set—RISC processor used for IPU
- Tailor microstep flow according to macro-instruction usage frequency—vector instruction set and vector pipes

Data-path cycle time: $t1$ (seconds/microcycle)

Ways used to decrease $t1$:
- Faster technology—ECL, high-speed CMOS and TTL
- Shorter physical data paths—VLSI components

Memory used per operation: $K2$ (bits/operation)

Ways used to decrease $K2$:
- Increase operand bits/instruction—vectors
- More efficient instruction set—vector instructions

Memory access time: $t2$ (seconds/bit)

Ways used to decrease $t2$:
- Faster technology
- Apparent speedup—I/D caches, TLBs, memory interleaving
- Widening word access—two 64-bit buses
- More efficient utilization of bandwidth—split transaction synchronous bus, prefetch, IPU write buffer

parameters of the model. The features are described in terms of the architectural implementation mechanisms presented in Chapter 2. As mentioned earlier, the system designer attempts to maximize throughput (the number of operations completed per second) and minimize latency (the amount of time required to start an operation).

The various techniques listed in Table 3.4 affect one or both of these performance metrics as depicted in Table 3.5; however, these techniques cannot be applied independently. For example, parallelism is represented by multiple functional units, multiprocessors, and pipelines, but parallelism requires a high bus and memory bandwidth so that data can be supplied rapidly enough to keep the parallel operations active. Thus, effective use of CPU parallelism is dependent on having sufficient memory bandwidth.

Table 3.5 illustrates the performance interdependencies in Titan. These features can be said to exhibit synergy, because supplying a single feature without improving interdependent features will yield little or no performance enhancement. Chapter 6 will illustrate the relationship between all these features in the Titan architecture.

There is also an interdependence between the predicted performance enhancement of the various techniques. For example, having two proces-

TABLE 3.5.   Interaction of principles.

Technique	Latency	Throughput	Synergism
$K1$ (microcycles/operation)			
More efficient instruction set	●	●	Bus/memory bandwidth
Multiple functional units, IPU, FPU		●	Bus/memory bandwidth
Multiprocessor		●	Bus/memory bandwidth
Pipelining		●	Bus/memory bandwidth, vectors
Vector registers	●	●	Bus/memory bandwidth
Vector Load pipe		●	Bus/memory bandwidth
C = A + B	●	●	Tailored data path
$K2$ (bits/operation)			
Vectors	●	●	Bus/memory bandwidth, pipelining
$t2$ (seconds/bit)			
Cache	●	●	Decreases need for bus/ memory bandwidth
Interleaving	●	●	Bus
Bus width	●	●	Memory bandwidth
Split bus	●	●	Memory bandwidth
Disconnected bus		●	Memory controller complexity

sors and doubling the bus memory bandwidth does not yield a factor of four (e.g., 2 × 2) improvement in system performance. The bus and memory bandwidth must be supplied to keep the two processors executing at their potential rate. Chapter 6 presents a model that takes into account these interdependencies.

3.3.3   STANDARD BENCHMARKS

A carefully designed standard benchmark gives the best estimate of real use, because the benchmark is totally understood and can be run on several different machines. A further advantage of standard benchmarks is that they are written in the high-level language to be used by the computer; hence they reflect the performance of the available compilers and operating systems as well as characterizing the machine architecture. Several organizations, especially those that purchase or use many machines extensively, have one or more programs characteristic of their own particular workload. Whether a standard benchmark is of value in characterizing performance depends on the degree to which it is typical of the actual computer's use.

The strongest advantage of the benchmark scheme is that it can handle a total problem and integrate all features of the computer. But there is a difficulty. The result depends not only on the type of computer (e.g., an IBM 3090), but on the exact configuration (e.g., the number of words of Mp) and even on the operating system and the software (e.g., the specific version of FORTRAN). Thus, although the benchmark performance number perhaps comes closest to serving as an adequate single performance figure, it is weaker as a parameter characterizing the structure of the computer than one characterizing a total system.

In particular, RISC integer processors are well known to derive greatly increased speed on benchmarks such as Dhrystone through the use of extremely sophisticated compiler techniques. While many of these compiler techniques are applicable to CISC machines such as the VAX family, such compilers were not in widespread usage when RISC results were first reported. Of course, RISC proponents claim that their architectures make it easier to write such sophisticated compilers, so the debate rages on.

In other words, it is quite fair and reasonable for the purchaser of a complete system to use standard benchmarks to evaluate performance; however, it may be unfair to evaluate an architecture's merits by using standard benchmarks in the presence of grossly inferior or superior compiler- and operating-system software technology or by using a stripped-down model of the system. In benchmarks, there are no absolutes, and the best advice is caveat emptor.

There are several widely used standardized benchmarks for both integer and vector instruction sets. The following benchmarks have been used for non-vector performance evaluation:

Whetstone (Curnow and Wichmann, 1976). A synthetic benchmark used to characterize FORTRAN scalar computational performance (which includes heavy use of floating-point computations), this test simulates high-level language patterns of use weighted by instruction types. Developed by the National Physical Laboratory in the United Kingdom, the Whetstone was carefully designed to be typical (e.g., frequencies of the trigonometric functions, subroutines, and I/O were considered).

Dhrystone (Weicker, 1984). Whereas the Whetstone attempts to capture typical scientific environments, the Dhrystone is aimed more at symbolic and integer processing. Also a synthetic benchmark, it was originally written in Ada but is more widely used in its C version. It is based on statistical data about the actual usage of programming language features in languages such as C and Pascal.

AIM benchmarks. Written in C, this test measures UNIX systems performance on a variety of levels. These tests include disk-file system, C compiler, multi-user sort, multi-user edit, word processing, data-base management, spread sheet, and accounting. Over 50 areas of system architecture are probed by these benchmarks.

ANSYS. Developed by Swanson Analysis Systems, this benchmark is a finite-element analysis program. It measures CPU, memory, and I/O resources.

Business benchmark. A multi-tasking benchmark which measures computer performance under 18 types of simulated work and over a range of up to 100 simultaneous tasks. Developed by Neal Nelson and Associates, the benchmark evaluates performance in both computational- and disk-intensive tasks in order to predict how a machine will perform with a large number of concurrent users.

There have also been a number of benchmarks designed for vector machines. This list includes:

LINPACK (Dongarra, 1989). This benchmark, developed by the Argonne National Laboratory, compares the ability of different computers to solve dense systems of linear equations in a FORTRAN environment. It is perhaps the most widely reported measure of floating-point computations on supercomputers and is widely regarded as a fair measure of performance. LAPACK is a rewritten version of LINPACK that is specifically designed for machines with vector registers.

Livermore Loops (McMahon, 1986). A set of 24 FORTRAN routines designed to be representative of scientific computations.

NAS Kernel. A Numerical Aerodynamic Simulator developed by NASA/Ames.

Los Alamos Vector Operations. A set of FORTRAN loops composed of basic arithmetic operations between scalars and vectors.

EXAMPLE 3.3 Combining the results of multiple benchmarks.

Benchmarks are frequently composed of more than one program. How can the results of these programs be combined to yield a single number characterizing performance? The only legitimate metric is the time required to perform the specified computation. (Smith, 1988). Table 3.6 is an example from (Smith, 1988) depicting the performance of two programs on three different computers. Computer 3 is almost three times faster than Computer 2 and 25 times faster than Computer 1.

It is common practice to calculate the rate at which a computer performs computations. If each of the programs in Table 3.6 contained 100 million floating-point operations, the computational rates are given in

TABLE 3.6. Execution time of two programs on three different computers.

	Computer 1 Time (Sec)	Computer 2 Time (Sec)	Computer 3 Time (Sec)
Benchmark			
Program 1	1	10	20
Program 2	1000	100	20
Total Time	1001	110	40

TABLE 3.7. Execution rate of two programs on three different computers in MFLOPS.

	Computer 1	Computer 2	Computer 3
Benchmark			
Program 1	100	10	5
Program 2	0.1	1	5
Arithmetic mean	50.1	5.5	5
Geometric mean	3.2	3.2	5
Harmonic mean	0.2	1.8	5

Table 3.7. At least three different ways of combining computational rates have been suggested:

- Arithmetic mean. Sum the rates and divide by the number of programs (n).
- Geometric mean. Multiply the rates and take the nth root.
- Harmonic mean. Sum the reciprocals of the rates and divide the results into n.

For the example in Table 3.7, the arithmetic mean indicates that Computer 1 is ten times more powerful than Computer 3 even though Computer 3 finished the computation of both programs 25 times faster than Computer 1. The geometric mean rates Computer 1 and Computer 2 identical even though Computer 2 finished the computation in one-tenth the time. Only the harmonic mean produces the same ordering and relative performance as depicted in Table 3.6. A little algebraic manipulation demonstrates that harmonic mean is the total number of operations divided by total time.

$$\text{Harmonic mean} = n\Sigma(1/Ri)$$

where Ri is the computational rate of program i. But

$$Ri = Ni/Ti$$

where Ni is the total number of operations in program i and Ti is the time to execute program i. To simplify the discussion, assume Ni is the same for each program and equals N.
Hence:

$$\text{Harmonic mean} = n/\Sigma Ti/N$$
$$= nN/\Sigma Ti,$$

which is proportional to the total number of operations executed in all n programs divided by the total time to execute all n programs.

Thus (Smith, 1988) concludes the following:

- Use the arithmetic mean when comparing performance expressed as time. Do not use it to summarize performance expressed as a rate.
- Use the harmonic mean for summarizing performance expressed as a rate. It will correspond to the expected execution time of real programs.

If the actual program mix does not correspond to the benchmark mix, the results of each benchmark can be weighted proportionally to the frequency of occurrence in the program mix of the computation typified by that benchmark.

Consider a benchmark with 24 subprograms (such as the Livermore Loops). Due to the finely tuned nature of a pipelined processor, different subprograms can vary by an order of magnitude or more. Consider one subprogram that executes 25 times more slowly (or 1/25th the rate) than the average. If all other subprograms executed at rate R, the harmonic mean for the entire benchmark would be $2R$. Conversely, if that one subprogram executed infinitely fast, the harmonic mean would be $1.04R$. Since the subprograms are uniformly weighted and are thus not calibrated to the actual expected workload, a single subprogram that may not occur in practice may lead to a pessimistic indication of performance. Users must examine the nature of their workload and its correlation to the standard benchmarks.

Table 3.8 depicts the Titan P2's performance on the traditional uniprocessor benchmarks. Standard benchmarks are frequently composed of different subcomputations designed to stress different features of the architecture. Table 3.9 compares the scalar and vector performance of Titan model P2 and P3 as a function of vector operation and vector length. The following observations can be made:

Scalar. Performance in P3 increases as a function of vector length and then starts to decrease for long vectors. P2's performance degrades for long vectors only for arbitrary indexing of vectors (Loops 10, 11, 12, and 13). P3's performance is generally two to three times that of P2 (except for very long vectors).

Vector. Vector performance is greater than scalar performance; furthermore, performance increases as vector length increases, since the vector start-up overhead can be amortized over more vector elements. P2 experiences performance drop-offs for long vectors in Loops 10–13. P3 is generally one and one-half to two times higher performance than P2, except on Loops 10–13 where it is two to three times higher performance.

Chapter 7 explores how the Titan P3 model was improved over P2, especially in eliminating the bottlenecks in Loops 10–13.

TABLE 3.8.   Titan P2 single processor performance on standard benchmarks.

	Titan P2	Titan P3
Whetstones		
MWhetstones/s	6.5	19
Dhrystone		
KDhyrstone/s	23	51
Livermore Loops	1.84	4.5
LINPACK (100 × 100)		
MFLOPS	6.5	10

TABLE 3.9. Los Alamos vector operations.

Loop Number	Scalar (MFLOPS)					
	P2 Vector Length			P3 Vector Length		
	10	100	1000	10	100	1000
1) V = V + S	1.29	1.51	1.54	3.19	3.54	1.60
2) V = S * V	1.3	1.51	1.53	3.0	3.28	1.52
3) V = V + V	0.82	0.94	0.96	2.31	2.82	0.86
4) V = V * V	0.81	0.95	0.96	2.16	2.58	0.84
5) V = V + S * V	1.52	1.77	1.81	3.34	3.82	1.45
6) V = V * V + S	1.27	1.45	1.49	3.34	3.82	1.46
7) V = V + V + V	1.12	1.28	1.32	2.63	3.23	1.04
8) V = S * V + SW	1.19	1.30	1.32	3.99	4.47	1.99
9) V = V * V + V * V	0.80	0.85	0.85	2.89	3.32	1.06
10) V = V(IND) + S	1.19	1.46	1.14	2.27	2.60	1.06
11) V(IND) = V * V	0.87	1.01	0.87	1.86	2.15	0.63
12) V(IND) = V(IND) + V * V	1.11	1.21	0.81	2.24	2.09	0.76
13) V = V + V * V(IND)	1.15	1.34	1.25	2.67	3.22	0.89
14) S = S + V	1.84	2.29	2.34	4.58	5.38	2.44
15) V = V/V	0.47	0.52	0.53	1.22	1.34	0.68
16) V = SQRT(V)	0.11	0.11	0.11	0.42	0.42	0.38
Harmonic Mean	0.66	0.72	0.70	1.92	2.10	0.95
Average	1.05	1.22	1.18	2.63	3.01	1.17

Loop Number	Vector (MFLOPS)					
	P2 Vector Length			P3 Vector Length		
	10	100	1000	10	100	1000
1) V = V + S	3.16	5.50	5.91	4.8	10.67	13.06
2) V = S * V	3.07	5.42	5.85	4.8	10.67	13.02
3) V = V + V	2.69	4.28	4.61	4.26	6.91	7.56
4) V = V * V	2.68	4.28	4.59	4.26	6.85	7.47
5) V = V + S * V	4.23	6.90	7.30	6.28	10.97	12.15
6) V = V * V + S	4.08	7.10	7.59	6.40	10.93	12.15
7) V = V + V + V	4.00	5.84	6.26	6.13	9.15	9.92
8) V = S * V + SW	4.97	8.00	8.52	9.60	16.69	18.28
9) V = V * V + V * V	4.20	5.35	5.48	6.40	9.15	9.77
10) V = V(IND) + S	1.34	1.90	1.37	2.49	3.56	3.81
11) V(IND) = V * V	1.64	2.38	1.59	2.13	2.71	2.86
12) V(IND) = V(IND) + V * V	1.59	2.11	1.01	2.26	2.94	3.06
13) V = V + V * V(IND)	2.19	2.76	2.15	3.41	4.47	4.68
14) S = S + V	2.03	4.28	4.81	2.77	5.82	6.73
15) V = V/V	0.48	0.51	0.51	2.67	3.10	3.20
16) V = SQRT(V)	0.31	0.35	0.36	1.62	1.77	1.78
Harmonic Mean	1.48	1.90	1.73	3.50	4.98	5.30
Average	2.67	4.19	4.24	4.42	7.27	8.09

3.4   THE IMPORTANCE OF BALANCE

The central issue in designing cost-effective computers is one of balance. A good computer architecture achieves a balance between system complexity and performance. A well-balanced architecture's subsystems are designed to have roughly comparable capacities for control and data movement. For example, the processing units with the system should not require more memory bandwidth for data than is available, nor should controller units lag behind the resources that they are controlling.

The reason for desiring this balance is that if any one subsystem has diminished capacity with respect to the others it forms a system performance bottleneck. Also, if any subsystem has a much greater capacity than the rest of the system, it probably cost more to build than was necessary. There is, of course, a valid need to build excess capacity into subsystems like data buses to provide for enhancement of other portions of the system, but this too should be held in line with reasonable expectations of future requirements.

Kiviat graphs are one way to graphically represent balance. In a Kiviat graph, if the various spokes of the wheel are approximately of the same length (and on the same scale), then the system is fairly well balanced. We have seen that the Titan and Cray Kiviat graphs have similar ratios among elements of their graphs and that the graphs are balanced. As we examine the performance of Titan in Chapter 6, we shall see how the various elements of the architecture come into play to achieve this balance. But first Chapter 4 will present how the various aspects of the Titan architecture support a typical application.

HIERARCHICAL
MODEL OF
COMPUTATION

In this chapter, we shall build a simple model of computation for a graphics supercomputer. For each level of the model, we shall discuss how concurrency and specialization may be used to increase performance, using Titan as an example. The goal is to explain how and why Titan uses general techniques of concurrency before a detailed explanation of the design of Titan is given in the next chapter.

4.1   A HIGH-LEVEL MODEL OF COMPUTATION

A graphics supercomputer is designed to take input data, perform many computations, and display the results as a high-quality graphics image. Figure 4.1 shows this high-level model of computation.

4.1.1 PHASES OF THE HIGH-LEVEL MODEL

In the high-level model, execution of a program begins with an operating system phase, during which initial resources are allocated, the program is loaded into memory, and execution begins. Actual program execution starts with an input phase, during which the data set for the program is read in. This is followed by a computation phase, during which the data

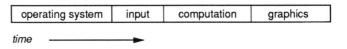

FIGURE 4.1.   A high-level model of a typical scientific computation.

set is transformed into the desired results. The final step is the graphics
display phase, in which the results undergo transformation into a suitable
graphics image.

4.1.2 HIGH-LEVEL CONCURRENCY

On small computers, all phases of the program execution are often handled by a single processor. This yields a simple system but does not result
in very high performance. The problem is that a processor designed for
integer arithmetic and logical control is not well suited for specialized tasks
such as floating-point computation and graphics manipulations. In all but
the lowest performance systems, specialized hardware is used to speed up
important classes of operations. The most widespread example is that of
the floating-point coprocessor chips used with personal computers.

In Titan, concurrency by replication and specialization is used to
increase the computation rate. Using multiple CPUs allows breaking the
problem into sub-problems to be solved concurrently on separate CPUs.
Of course, having specialized hardware to support floating-point computations and graphics rendering also speeds execution.

Having a separate IPU, VPU, and GPU allows some aspects of input,
computation, and graphics to be overlapped. In many cases, the first few
results of a computation may be passed to the GPU for display even while
more results are being calculated. An even simpler example is that of animation, where different pictures in the animation sequence can be in different phases of processing (for example, one picture being displayed, the
next being drawn, the next being computed, the next having raw data read,
and the next being scheduled by the operating system).

4.2   A MORE DETAILED MODEL OF COMPUTATION

Titan approaches the problem of providing specialized hardware for
important functions with the philosophy of providing the minimum
required hardware consistent with high speed performance. As we have
seen, graphics supercomputing requires four phases. Figure 4.2 shows

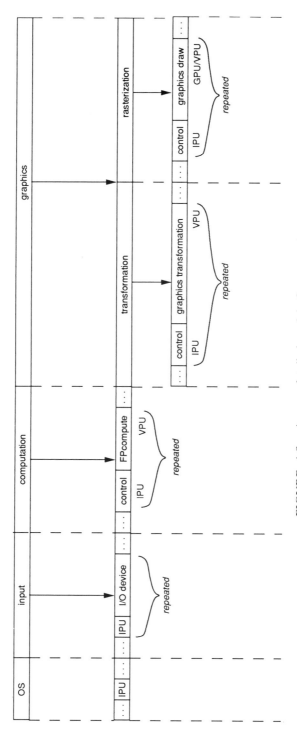

FIGURE 4.2. A more detailed model of computation.

99

how each of these phases may be broken into smaller parts that are mapped onto different processing subsystems within Titan. Each set of elisions in the figure indicates that the sequence is repeated as often as required within the segment (for example, the computation phase consists of repeated pairs of "control" and "floating-point compute" operations).

4.2.1   THE PIECES OF THE MODEL

The operating system phase requires a general-purpose integer processor unit (IPU). This role should be filled well by any standard processor.

The input phase requires high-speed I/O support, so Titan has an I/O subsystem for interfacing to non-graphics peripherals. The IPU is the control unit for this subsystem. The input phase therefore consists of repeated instances of the IPU performing control functions to set up an I/O transfer, followed by the I/O device responding to the transfer request under guidance from the I/O controller.

The computation phase usually involves floating-point arithmetic. For this reason, Titan has a sophisticated Vector floating Point unit (VPU) with hardware support for floating-point multiplication, addition, and division. However, the computation phase also requires a significant amount of bookkeeping such as array address generation and conditional branching. Titan uses the IPU as a control unit to the VPU to provide these services.

The graphics display phase actually consists of two subphases: transformation and rasterization. The transformation subphase consists of what really amounts to another computation phase, during which high-quality rendering algorithms and 3D graphics transformations (coordinate transformations and perspective calculations) are computed by the IPU and VPU. The rasterization subphase (during which the data is converted from three-dimensional point sets to actual pixel color and intensity values) consists of the IPU acting as the control processor for specialized graphics hardware in the GPU.

4.2.2   CONCURRENCY IN THE DETAILED MODEL

At a more detailed model level, the opportunities for concurrency seem even more evident. Within each subphase of the computation, sequences of control and processing are repeated. If the control phase for the next stage of the repetition can be overlapped with the computation phase, then a major speed improvement is possible. This is exactly what is done in Titan.

A classic example of overlap in most high-performance computers is that of I/O and computation. In the input phase, the IPU initiates a block memory transfer which is controlled by the I/O processing logic. This frees the IPU either to process data already read in or set up buffers for the next input function.

In the computation and graphics transformation phases, the IPU control functions may be overlapped with the VPU computation phases. This is accomplished in Titan by using a buffer between the IPU and the VPU. This buffer holds vector instructions issued by the IPU until the VPU is ready to execute them.

In the graphics rasterization phase, the IPU operation can be overlapped with the GPUs rendering operations. This is accomplished by using main memory as a buffer between the IPU and the GPU. The IPU builds a data structure containing commands for the GPU (called a display list). When the list is ready, the IPU initiates the GPU execution of the list, freeing the IPU for other work. If a single picture is broken up into a sequence of display lists, the IPU and GPU may overlap their processing on the same picture.

Another level of concurrency is possible in the graphics portion of the processing. If two CPUs are installed, one CPU may process the graphics transformations while another CPU processes the rasterization. In some high-quality rasterization processes, the VPU is needed in addition to the GPU, so this represents an area where two CPUs can be completely used in parallel. In actual practice, rasterization can be so computationally expensive that one CPU can be dedicated to performing all phases except rasterization (OS, input, computation, and transformation) while the other CPU performs the rasterization functions. This same strategy may be extended to assigning a number of CPUs to each task, or even completely separate machines (with multiple CPUs) to the tasks.

4.2.3 HARDWARE REUSE IN TITAN

The reader will immediately notice the reuse of subsystems (especially the IPU) for the various phases of the problems. In a cost-is-no-object system with maximum throughput as the only goal, each phase of computation would have dedicated, optimized hardware. However, Titan was conceived as a system which achieves the best possible speed with limited hardware resources. This means that the computation problem must be divided in a way that extracts as much use out of the available hardware as possible, even at the expense of a moderate increase in the complexity of the control hardware and software.

The reason that Titan's reuse of hardware makes sense is that the desired goal is speedup for a single problem. That means that resources may be reused in different phases of the computation without compromising system performance. Thus, anytime an integer-based control processor is needed, the IPU is reused. This occurs in every phase of the computation. Floating-point computations are needed twice: once to perform problem computations and once to perform graphics transformations. While separate floating point transformation hardware can be and often is built into graphics display hardware, this represents a waste of resources if the same floating-point hardware can be reused as it is in Titan.

So what we see in Titan is a tempering of the overlapped computation possibilities with the realities of economics. The possibility of adding multiple CPUs eliminates the disadvantages to a large degree, because added IPU/VPU pairs can permit overlap between phases. The minimum level system need only have a small amount of hardware, with incremental upgrades of general-purpose modules giving improved performance.

4.3   PRIMITIVE OPERATIONS

There is yet another level in the hierarchy of performance modeling: that of processes common to all segments of the system. These processes are instruction execution and memory access (for which each in turn has smaller subcomponents). Since all functional units of Titan perform these operations, we shall describe them once in a general manner, with the understanding that they apply with slight modification to all computation phases in the previous layers of the hierarchy.

4.3.1   INSTRUCTION EXECUTION

The fetch/decode/execute instruction cycle is common to all conventional processors. Each subsystem executes a sequence of instructions whenever it is invoked in a computation. Figure 4.3 shows the breakdown of what happens for each instruction. Each instruction must be fetched, be decoded, have its data fetched, execute, then have its results stored.[1] This

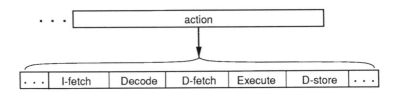

FIGURE 4.3.   Instruction execution model.

[1] The instruction and operand address generation phases from Figure 2.10 are assumed overlapped with other computation and are deleted from Figure 4.3.

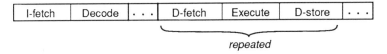

FIGURE 4.4.   Vector instruction execution model.

sequence is repeated for as many instructions as are necessary for the IPU, VPU, or GPU to accomplish its task. Actually, it is often possible to break down the sequence of events further depending on the specifics of a processor, but this is an appropriate level for a generic model.

Changes in the model for the various functional units of Titan are few and obvious. For example, Figure 4.4 shows that the VPU only needs a single I-fetch and Decode for each vector instruction, followed by a repeating sequence of D-fetch/execute/D-store operations.

4.3.2   MEMORY ACCESS

A further level of breakdown within instruction execution is possible because each reference to memory may result in a cache or virtual memory miss that requires still more processing. Figure 4.5 shows this process.

If the required memory element is kept in a cache, then it is accessed immediately. If it is not in cache, a cache miss procedure is executed by hardware. This results in a further decision being made: whether the data is in physical memory or in a virtual memory page that is not currently resident in memory. If the data is in physical memory, a memory access cycle is initiated. If not, the operating system is invoked to process the page fault (which in turn executes instructions that perform memory accesses).

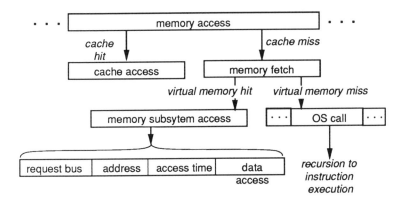

FIGURE 4.5.   Memory access model.

At this point we have a model of the computation that breaks program execution into layers, the lowest levels of which form a sequence of machine operations. We have observed that Titan makes judicious use of specialized hardware subsystems in the form of the IPU, VPU, GPU, and I/O Unit to speed up the execution phase of each instruction.

Now we are armed with a feel for how and why a high-performance scientific processor is designed the way it is. In the next chapter, we shall examine in detail the design of the Titan architecture.

TITAN ARCHITECTURE AND ITS IMPLEMENTATION

In this chapter, we shall examine the Titan architecture in detail. At this point, we have enough background knowledge of how the system should be organized for high performance to examine exactly how these techniques are implemented and how they are merged at the hardware level.

As previously shown in Figure 1.2, Titan has several major functional blocks: the system bus, memory, the Integer-Processing Unit (IPU), the Vector-Processing Unit (VPU), the Graphics-Processing Unit (GPU), and the I/O processor. We shall examine them all in turn.

5.1 SYSTEM BUS

The heart of Titan is the system bus. The fact that it is a global bus provides great advantages as well as the fundamental limit to system speed. The strength comes from the ability to install multiple processors without having to concern the software with data partitioning and access strategies. These concerns can greatly complicate matters in a system with local processor memory. The limit to speed comes when multiple VPUs, combined with other system resources, saturate the bus with memory access requests.

The system bus uses both redundancy and pipelining to accomplish speedup. The redundancy in the system bus follows from the use of two data transfer buses: the S-BUS and the R-BUS. This provides two paths into the system memory, doubling the amount of memory bandwidth available to the rest of the system.

The S-BUS (Store Bus) is a read/write bus that is used for general-purpose access to memory. All access to memory from the IPU, GPU, and I/O subsystem use the S-BUS. Additionally, all vector writes from the VPU to memory use the S-BUS as well.

The R-BUS is a second bus used only for reading from memory by vector processors in support of high-speed operand fetches. As we shall see later, the demands upon memory made by a VPU are very high and merit a separate bus just for vector reads.

The S-BUS and the R-BUS have a bandwidth of 128 MB-per-second each. This gives the system a 256 MB-per-second memory access rate. Each bus uses a split transaction protocol. This means that in the case of a read from memory, the requester first asserts an address and then relinquishes use of the bus until the data is ready to be returned.

Transactions on both the S-BUS and the R-BUS follow the pattern shown in Figure 5.1. Each bus cycle begins with the requester examining a set of BUSY lines to see if the desired resource is available. There is one BUSY line for each interleave of memory, so a memory requester decodes the interleave number of interest and examines that interleave's BUSY line. This scheme prevents wasting bus cycles by attempting to access an unavailable resource or having to queue requests at the memory.

Once the requester finds the resource it needs available, it spends a clock cycle requesting the resource and a bus cycle using it. When the request is granted, the requester drives the address onto the address lines of the bus.

The requester then waits two or more cycles for the data to be available. In the delay between the address and the data read, other subsystems (or even the same requester for a subsequent piece of data) are allowed to use the bus to access other memory addresses. Then the data is taken from the bus-data lines in two half-word (32-bit) pieces on successive cycles. The first half-word is taken from the "Data Lo" data lines of the bus, the sec-

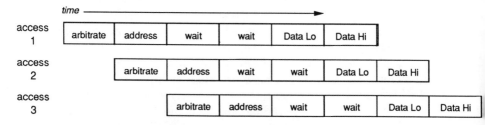

FIGURE 5.1. Titan bus read cycles.

ond half-word from the "Data Hi" data lines. The reason for splitting the data into two halves is discussed in detail in the memory subsystem section. Because no signal lines on the bus are asserted for more than one clock cycle, bus accesses may be pipelined, with one bus access being initiated per clock cycle.

Some of the bus requesters, such as the vector load and store pipes, can issue multiple memory references. This request-ahead behavior allows multiple active memory requests over the bus from a single functional unit, thus accomplishing overlap of memory accesses. Both these kinds of overlap correspond to the memory subsystem access overlap shown in Figure 4.5.

This bus bandwidth will ultimately limit the number of processors that may be usefully employed in Titan. It is important to note that a significant effort was made to speed this bus up as much as possible consistent with cost constraints. For example, all bus handshaking signals use Emitter-Coupled Logic (ECL) for maximum speed, while the data lines are high-speed Transistor–Transistor Logic (FAST series TTL). ECL logic is very fast but has demanding power and cooling requirements. FAST series TTL is slower than ECL but is much easier to work with, takes less power, and costs less to build. A more detailed description of the bus is given in Appendix C.

5.2 MEMORY

Titan uses a full memory hierarchy consisting of registers, cache memories, physical memory, and virtual memory. The goal of all the memories is to provide the highest possible response bandwidth to requests for memory access while providing a very large memory space for software to use.

5.2.1 CACHE MEMORY

Titan uses two kinds of cache memory. The first kind is the split I- and D-cache found in the IPU. These caches provide high-speed response for instruction and data access, respectively, to the IPU. The size is 16K bytes per cache. The set size is one, with each word of memory mapping into exactly one cache location based on the lowest bits of the address. The block size of the MIPS IPU chip is 32 bits, or 4 bytes, although the effect of having a line size of 64 bits is simulated on Titan by using external hardware to support double-word fetches from the system bus to the cache.

The Titan IPU uses a write-through policy to maintain cache coherency. A bus-watcher circuit invalidates entries in the data cache if it observes that they have been written by another functional unit. The instruction cache has no such protection circuit (saving considerable hardware), on the assumption that programs are not self-modifying. On a cache miss, one word (32 bits) is fetched from memory if the address is on an odd word boundary, and two words (64 bits) are fetched if the address is on an even word boundary. This strategy allows the exploitation of spatial locality by prefetching one instruction ahead of the instruction being fetched.

Direct-mapped caches are used instead of set-associative caches because of their simplicity. While direct mapped memory usually has a lower hit rate than set-associative memory, the extra clock cycle time needed to process the associative memory lookup was not deemed a good tradeoff for Titan. This is because the lengthening of the clock cycle would slow the system down more than lost clock cycles caused by the slightly increased cache miss ratio experienced with a direct mapped cache (Przybylski *et al.*, 1988).

The second kind of cache in Titan is the Vector Register File (VRF) used in the VPU. The purpose of the VRF is to maintain locally accessible copies of data items needed by the VPU in high-speed memory. Thus, the VRF forms a software-managed cache of values. The VRF was included in the design instead of a regular cache because vector processors are notorious for having low hit ratios in standard cache schemes.

The IPU also has a TLB cache internal to the MIPS processor. The VPU has an External TLB cache (ETLB) that is managed in software by the IPU. The organization and performance of the IPU cache and the VRF are discussed further in Section 5.3.2.

5.2.2 PHYSICAL MEMORY

Titan uses from one to four memory boards and can provide a system memory of 8 MB to 128 MB. A block diagram of the memory board is shown in Figure 5.2.

The memory subsystem in Titan uses redundancy for speeding up program execution. Because there are multiple functional units that all compete for the use of program memory, it is quite reasonable to have multiple memory accesses active at the same time. These accesses are handled by using 8 (or 16) memory interleave controllers. Redundancy of access paths into memory is also supported so that the R-BUS and S-BUS can simultaneously access different interleaves.

Each memory board contains eight interleave controllers based on lowest-order bits of memory double-word (8 byte) addresses, each with between one and four banks of 256K × 4 bit dynamic RAM (DRAM) chips. Each interleave controller can take an address from either the S-BUS or

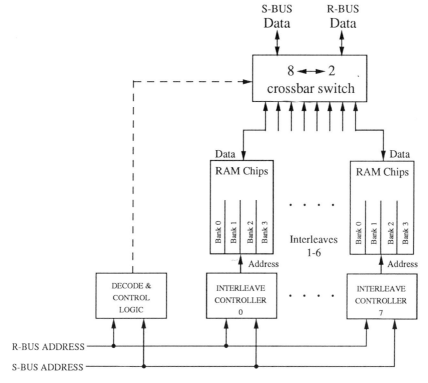

FIGURE 5.2.   Memory subsystem block diagram.

the R-BUS. The data sides of the DRAM chips are connected to an 8-to-2 crossbar switch which allows any two of the memory interleaves to be connected to either of the S-BUS or R-BUS simultaneously. Each memory board is capable of initiating two memory transactions per clock cycle (one on each bus), giving a dual-ported appearance to the system memory.

A single memory board with one bank of DRAM chips per interleave controller provides 8 MB of memory, giving up to 32 MB per card and 128 MB per four-memory-card Titan System. Provisions have been made for direct substitution of 1M × 4 bit DRAM chips to increase system memory capacity to 512 MB.

Because there are eight interleave controllers on each memory board, a single memory-board system cannot provide more than an eight-way interleaved memory. When pairs of boards with identical RAM chip configurations are installed, each board pair is accessed as a 16-way interleaved memory element, providing better performance. The performance improvement can in theory be up to a factor of two, if all 16 interleaves are active at the same time.

Figure 5.3 shows the sequence of events for performing a single read from memory operation. On the first clock cycle, the address decoding unit takes addresses from both the buses and decodes the interleave number for the addresses. Each interleave controller can only process one memory access at a time, so addresses must be guaranteed not to access a busy interleave. This guarantee is made by using the INTERLEAVE BUSY bus lines to prevent any processor from requesting memory cycles from a busy interleave.

On the next cycle, the interleave controller processes the address and determines which of the four banks of DRAM the request is for. The DRAM row/column address sequence is also started during this clock cycle. The third clock cycle of the sequence is spent waiting for the DRAM chips to access memory. The fourth clock cycle returns the low 32 bits of the result onto the system bus. In order to provide more interleaves for a minimum amount of memory chips (and therefore higher performance), the interleaves access memory as 32-bit-wide words. The "static column" capability of DRAM chips (i.e., the capability to access multiple data elements within a small range of addresses quickly) provides fast access to adjacent locations. Thus, the fifth clock cycle uses the static column mode to return the high 32 bits of the memory word from the same bank of 32-bit-wide DRAM chips. This feature accounts for the splitting of the high and low half of the value transmitted on the data bus. A final clock cycle is spent meeting DRAM chip precharge requirements before the memory is available for another cycle. This precharge time (t.recovery from Chapter 2) does not tie up the system bus, nor does it cause the receiver of the data to wait.

When the DRAM data is read, the interleave transmits its data through the crossbar switch (a half-word at a time) to the system bus, then is ready for the next access. The crossbar switch can actually handle four 32-bit quantities at a time: two low-half values from two banks, and two high-half values from two other banks.

The double-cycling of memory chips to access pairs of 32-bit quantities is the result of a tradeoff between access latency and memory bandwidth. Given that there is a limited amount of room on a board for memory and controller chips, Titan could have had four interleaves of 64 bits wide, or

address read from bus	interleave controller	wait	Data Lo	Data Hi	precharge

FIGURE 5.3. A memory cycle.

FIGURE 1. The Stardent 1500 "Titan" series graphics supercomputer: system overview. Copyright © 1988, Stardent Computer Inc.

FIGURE 2. The front of the system cabinet with a full ten-slot backplane, containing VME adapter, I/O, two cpu, four memory, graphics, and graphics expansion cards. Copyright © 1988, Stardent Computer Inc.

FIGURE 3. The back of the system cabinet showing the power and ground distribution to the system cards. Copyright © 1988, Stardent Computer Inc.

(a)

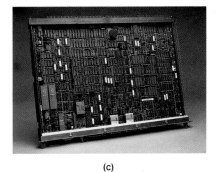

(b)   (c)

FIGURE 4. Details of three cards: (a) CPU, vector processor, and cache; (b) memory with eight interleave controllers; and (c) I/O. Copyright © 1988, Stardent Computer Inc.

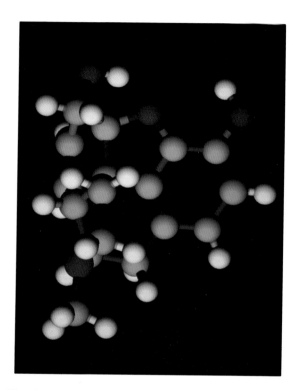

FIGURE 5. Chemists need a variety of rendering styles to focus on different molecular properties. The Molecular Simulator's™ visualization environment easily generates different representations of the same molecular data without recoding. This ball-and-stick image can also be rendered as a wireframe or ray-traced image. Data courtesy of BioDesign Inc. The Molecular Simulator is a trademark of Stardent Computer Corporation. Copyright © 1988, Stardent Computer Inc.

FIGURE 6. A 3-D helicopter rotor wake, rendered by Doré. In computational fluid dynamics applications, the full range of colors available from Doré can be used to represent pressure, velocity, temperature, vorticity, or other conditions. Copyright © 1988, Stardent Computer Inc.

FIGURE 7. The Newell teapot, rendered in 3-D, full color with the Doré integral ray tracer. The Doré toolkit allows the user to vary image realism as a function of computation time. Copyright © 1988, Stardent Computer Inc.

eight interleaves of 32 bits wide (cycled twice per access to simulate 64-bit width access) on each memory card. The double-cycling approach was chosen to double the available memory bandwidth at a cost of one clock cycle in additional access latency.

Titan's memory subsystem not only provides standard read and write functions, but also provides a synchronization primitive at the memory board level to avoid the need to lock the bus while providing an indivisible read/modify/write operation. The LOAD-AND-SYNC primitive reads the contents of the specified memory word, then increments the word if negative or sets it to zero if non-negative. If the LOAD-AND-SYNC primitive were not provided at the memory board level, there could be a severe performance penalty. This is because an indivisible modification primitive is required for synchronization, and the most obvious other option would be to wait for a round trip to the IPU from the memory to modify the element, tying up the memory interleave being modified for many clock cycles. Example 5.1 shows the operation of the LOAD-AND-SYNC instruction.

5.2.3 VIRTUAL MEMORY

All memory accesses performed by the IPU and VPU are to virtual memory addresses. Both the IPU and VPU contain Translation-Lookaside Buffers (TLBs) to map virtual addresses into physical addresses. All data-bus transactions and I/O are performed on real addresses. Titan uses disk drives attached to the SCSI (Small Computer System Interface standard) port of the I/O processor for virtual memory paging.

The TLB used by the IPU is built into the MIPS R2000 architecture. It contains 64 entries, with each entry corresponding to a 4 KB page of physical memory.

The TLB used by the vector unit (the ETLB discussed in the cache section) has 8096 entries, each corresponding to a 4 KB page of physical memory. All accesses to memory from the VPU are translated by the ETLB.

5.3 INTEGER UNIT

In most cases, Titan's Integer Processing Unit (IPU) performs merely as a controller for other system resources. The IPU often does not do much "real work" in the sense of producing actual computational results except when running Unix utilities and development tools such as editors and compilers; however, the IPUs efficiency is crucial because if it is not fast

---

EXAMPLE 5.1.   Operation of the LOAD-AND-SYNC primitive.

The LOAD-AND-SYNC primitive is the atomic memory updating operation supported by Titan. It works by reading the value at a memory location, and then (before the memory board hardware allows any other access to that location) performing a conditional increment operation. If the previous memory value was negative, the value read is incremented by one and written back to memory. If the previous memory value was non-negative, a zero is written to memory.

A simple application of LOAD-AND-SYNC is to dispatch portions of a loop to different processors. For example, the following code

```
        DO 100 I = 1,1000
        DO 200 J = 1,1000
        X(I,J) = Y(I,J) * Z(I)
200 CONTINUE
100 CONTINUE
```

could be broken up among parallel processors by dispatching each iteration of the inner loop to a different processor in a multi-processor Titan configuration. Some sort of synchronization mechanism would be needed to ensure that each iteration of the loop was performed exactly once. In order to accomplish this, the compiler would automatically issue the following code to each processor:

```
300 CONTINUE
        I = -SYNC(INDEX)
        IF ( I .EQ. 0 ) 100
        DO 200 J = 1,1000
            X(I,J) = Y(I,J) * Z(I)
200 CONTINUE
        GOTO 300
100 CONTINUE
```

where SYNC(INDEX) is a function that returns the value of a shared variable called INDEX that is accessed using the LOAD-AND-SYNC instruction. Note that this actual FORTRAN code would never really appear, since the compiler would produce assembly language output.

The behavior of this code is to use the negation of INDEX as the index for the inner loop. INDEX counts from its initial value of -1000 (set by the master processor before control is passed to the multiple processors) to 0, with an increment performed each time a processor reads a value for use as the variable I. Once INDEX has been incremented to 0, all the work is done and the multiple processors can begin other code.

enough at performing overhead and control operations, other system resources will have to wait for their instructions.

The IPU shown in Figure 5.4 is built around the MIPS R2000 Reduced Instruction Set Computer (RISC) processor. The R2000 has an internal Translation Lookaside Buffer (TLB) and supports split Instruction and Data caches (the I-Cache and the D-cache). In addition, Titan uses read and write buffers to interface the IPU to the system bus and has a bus watcher to maintain cache coherency in the Data cache.

5.3.1 MIPS ARCHITECTURE

The MIPS R2000 (Kane, 1987) is a heavily pipelined Reduced Instruction Set Computer (RISC) that is optimized to execute one instruction per clock cycle with an operating speed of 16 MHz. Among the features of the R2000 processor are

- A five-stage instruction execution pipeline,
- Thirty-two 32-bit general-purpose registers,
- Support for separate instruction and data caches,

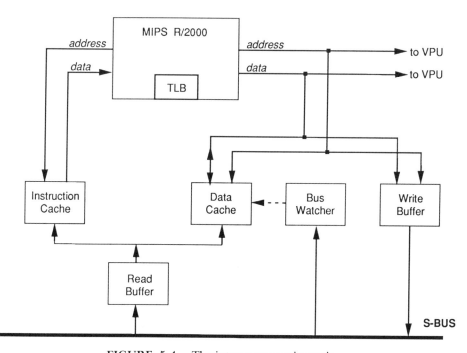

FIGURE 5.4.   The integer processing unit.

- Support for a memory write buffer, and
- An on-chip Translation Lookaside Buffer (TLB) of 64 elements for virtual memory support with a 4 KB page size.

The floating-point coprocessor for the R2000 is not used on the first version of Titan, since the VPU can perform all required floating-point operations.

Figure 5.5 shows the three instruction formats used by the R2000: the R-type (register-instruction type), the I-type (immediate data-instruction type), and the J-type (jump type). The register-instruction type is a three-address instruction, specifying two source registers (r-source and r-target) as well as a separate destination register (r-dest). The immediate-instruction type allows substituting a 16-bit immediate data field for the r-dest operand. Jump instructions specify a word-aligned target address for the jump, so the target field is shifted left two bits before being used as an actual address.

Since the R2000 is a RISC, there are a relatively small number of opcodes in the instruction set, each with only a single instruction format. Most operations are performed on registers, with the load and store instructions allowing access to memory-resident operands. Table 5.1 shows the instruction set of the MIPS R2000 processor. Each opcode is associated with a single instruction type.

All jump and branch instructions have a one-slot branch delay, meaning that the instruction just after a branch in a program is always executed (due to prefetching of instructions and partial execution of the following

R - type (*Register*)

31 26	25 21	20 16	15 11	10 6	5 0
Opcode	r-source	r-target	r-dest	shift	function

I- type (*Immediate*)

31 26	25 21	20 16	15 0
Opcode	r-source	r-target	immediate data

J - type (*jump*)

31 26	25 0
Opcode	target

FIGURE 5.5. R2000 instruction formats.

TABLE 5.1.   R2000 instruction summary.

OPCODE	TYPE	Description
		Arithmetic Instructions
ADD	R	ADD
ADDI	I	ADD Immediate
ADDIU	I	ADD Immediate Unsigned
ADDU	R	ADD Unsigned
AND	R	AND
ANDI	I	AND Immediate
NOR	R	Not-OR (logical "nor")
OR	R	OR
ORI	I	OR Immediate
SLT	R	Set Less Than
SLTI	I	Set on Less Than Immediate
SLTIU	I	Set on Less Than Immediate Unsigned
SLTU	R	Set Less Than Unsigned
SUB	R	SUBtract
SUBU	R	SUBtract Unsigned
XOR	R	eXclusive OR
XORI	I	eXclusive OR Immediate
		Shift Instructions
SLL	R	Shift Left Logical
SLLV	R	Shift Left Logical Variable
SRA	R	Shift Right Arithmetic
SRAV	R	Shift Right Arithmetic Variable
SRL	R	Shift Right Logical
SRLV	R	Shift Right Logical Variable
		Multiply/Divide Instructions
DIV	R	DIVide
DIVU	R	DIVide Unsigned
MFHI	R	Move From HI
MFLO	R	Move From LO
MTHI	R	Move To HI
MTLO	R	Move To LO
MULT	R	MULTiply
MULTU	R	MULTiply Unsigned
		Load/Store Instructions
LB	I	Load Byte
LBU	I	Load Byte Unsigned
LH	I	Load Halfword
LHU	I	Load Halfword Unsigned
LUI	I	Load Upper Immediate

TABLE 5.1. R2000 instruction summary (continued).

OPCODE	TYPE	Description
LW	I	Load Word
LWL	I	Load Word Left
LWR	I	Load Word Right
SB	I	Store Byte
SH	I	Store Halfword
SW	I	Store Word
SWL	I	Store Word Left
SWR	I	Store Word Right

Jump and Branch Instructions

BEQ	I	Branch on EQual
BGEZ	I	Branch on Greater than or Equal to Zero
BGEZAL	I	Branch on Greater than or Equal to Zero And Link
BGTZ	I	Branch on Greater Than Zero
BLEZ	I	Branch on Less than or Equal to Zero
BLTZ	I	Branch on Less Than Zero
BLTZAL	I	Branch on Less Than Zero And Link
BNE	I	Branch on Not Equal
J	J	Jump
JAL	J	Jump And Link
JALR	R	Jump And Link Register
JR	R	Jump to Register

Coprocessor Instructions

BCzF	I	Branch on Coprocessor z False
BCzT	I	Branch on Coprocessor z True
CFCz	R	move Control From Coprocessor z
COPz	R	Coprocessor z OPeration
CTCz	R	move Control to Coprocessor z
LWCz	I	Load Word from Coprocessor z
MFCz	R	Move From Coprocessor z
MTCz	R	Move To Coprocessor z
SWCz	I	Store Word to Coprocessor z

System Control Coprocessor Instructions

MFC0	R	Move From CP0
MTC0	R	Move To CP0
RFE	R	Restore From Exception
TLBP	R	TLB matching entry Probe
TLBR	R	TLB entry Read (indexed)
TLBWI	R	TLB entry Write (Indexed)
TLBWR	R	TLB entry Write (Random)

Special Instructions

BREAK	R	BREAK
SYSCALL	R	SYStem CALL

116

instruction in the pipeline prior to knowing that the branch will be taken). The assembler ensures that "safe" instructions are scheduled to fill this branch delay slot. If an instruction cannot be scheduled to fill the slot, a nop (no operation) must be inserted by the assembler.

The R2000 does not have a condition code register. Therefore, all conditional branch instructions are accomplished by comparing the contents of two data registers and branching if the comparison specified is true (e.g., branch if the two registers are equal). In some cases the second register for the comparison is implicitly register 0, which has a fixed value of 0.

All load operations are delayed by one clock cycle, meaning that the results of a register loaded from memory are not available to the instruction after the load. Once again, the assembler tries to squeeze a useful instruction in this load delay slot but issues a nop if useful work cannot be done.

The MIPS R2000, like other RISC processors, aggressively pipelines the sequence shown in Figure 4.3 to strive for an execution rate of one instruction per clock cycle. This includes overlapped instruction fetching, decoding, and execution, as well as separate buses for data fetching and instruction fetching. The limits that bar achieving the ideal of one clock cycle per instruction are data dependencies in the program, the response time of the memory hierarchy, and TLB misses.

5.3.2 INSTRUCTION/DATA CACHE

We have already discussed the memory hierarchy in general. Now let us examine the cache level of the memory hierarchy as it applies to the IPU.

The MIPS processor requires the use of two caches, one for data and one for instructions. This allows the processor to access both data and an instruction in the same clock cycle for a peak instruction execution rate of one instruction per clock cycle. The specific characteristics of the caches have already been discussed.

Since there are multiple processing elements in the system, the IPU must deal with the problem of cache coherence. This is accomplished by providing a bus watcher that maintains consistency within the D-cache whenever a bus write cycle is performed by any subsystem on Titan. In order to keep the cache coherency protocol simple, the D-cache is treated as write-through. In practice, this means that every memory write is sent both to the Data Cache and to the write buffer for writing into system memory.

IPU cache access can proceed in parallel with cache and virtual memory hit/miss determination. Techniques to accomplish this are described by Stone (1987) and are beyond the scope of this discussion.

5.3.3 IPU/VPU INTERFACE

In addition to normal control and integer scalar operations, the IPU is responsible for controlling the Vector Processing Unit. This is accomplished by having a special range of memory addresses for the IPU that map into the VPU control logic instead of memory. In this way the IPU can use store instructions to issue commands to the VPU as well as provide services when the VPU has an ETLB miss.

Floating-point instructions are issued by the IPU to the VPU by performing a 32-bit write to the Vector Control Unit (VCU). At peak processing rate, the IPU can issue a scalar floating-point instruction every second clock cycle, which corresponds to one floating-point instruction per VPU cycle.

There is a seven-element buffer between the IPU and the VPU to allow the IPU to initiate several VPU instructions and then proceed with further work while the VPU performs its computations. If the buffer between the IPU and VPU becomes full, the IPU is stalled until the buffer is emptied by the VPU.

5.4   VECTOR PROCESSING UNIT

The Vector Processing Unit (VPU), shown in Figure 5.6, provides the computational power that does the "real work" for both the computation and display phases of a program's execution on Titan. The VPU consists of a Vector Control Unit (VCU), a Vector Data Switch (VDS), a Vector Data Path (VDP), and a Vector Register File (VRF). The VPU can operate on 32- or 64-bit integer and floating-point vectors, with scalars treated as one-element vectors.

The vector processing unit has an overall clock rate of 8 MHz, which is one-half the clock rate of the IPU; however, we shall discuss several areas where individual activities within the VPU can happen on 16 MHz clock edges to keep all resources busy.

5.4.1   VECTOR DATA PATH

The VDP is the heart of the VPU, shown in Figure 5.7. The VDP contains a pipelined floating-point 64-bit ALU and a pipelined floating point 64-bit multiplier. Both the ALU and the multiplier have three pipeline stages and a latency of six clock cycles. Each pipeline stage takes two 16 MHz clocks to progress, giving an effective pipelined execution rate of 8 MHz.

Both the multiplier and the ALU may be active simultaneously, each providing eight million floating point operations per second (8 MFLOPS)

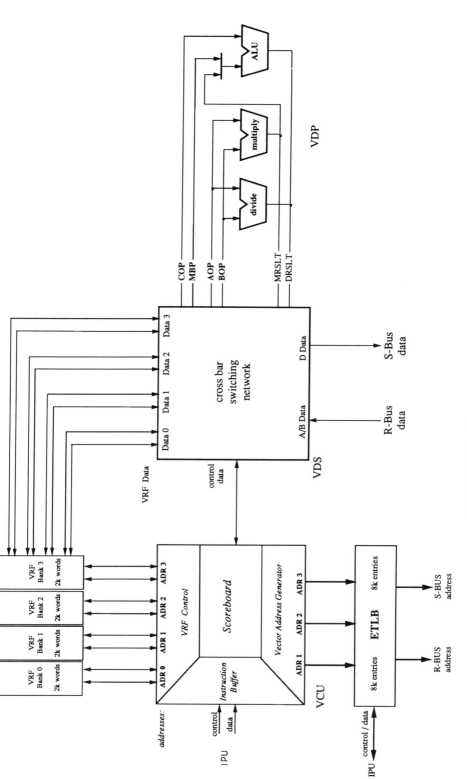

FIGURE 5.6. The vector processing unit.

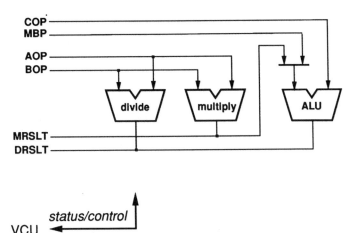

FIGURE 5.7.   The vector data path.

for a total of 16 MFLOPS. The inputs to the multiplier are the AOP and BOP inputs to the VDP. If a multiply–accumulate instruction is being processed for an application such as inner-product computation, the output of the multiplier is routed to the ALU along with the COP input. The ALU and multiplier may also be run independently by using the multiplexer on the left ALU input to select the MBP (Multiplier ByPass) input to the VDP. The multiplier's result is fed out of the VDP using the MRSLT output, and the ALU result using the DRSLT output.

A nonpipelined double precision divider is also included in the VDP to provide a 0.76 MFLOPS peak division rate with a latency of 16 16-MHz clocks. The peak single precision division rate is 1 MFLOPS.

All three functional units within the VDP can operate on 32-bit and 64-bit IEEE-standard floating-point numbers. They can also operate on 32-bit two's complement integers for high-speed integer arithmetic.

We can see from the description of the VDP that Titan uses three techniques to speed up arithmetic processing at the lowest level: specialization, replication and pipelining. The specialization comes from the fact that dedicated units are provided for multiplication and division. The replication comes from the fact that three hardware floating-point units are provided in the VDP (in this case the distinction between replication and specialization is rather blurry). Pipelining is used within the ALU and the multiplier to allow three operations to be in progress simultaneously within each unit.

5.4.2   VECTOR REGISTER FILE

Something must be done to satisfy the VDP's voracious demand for data, which, as we shall see in the next chapter, can exceed the bandwidth available from Titan's system bus. Traditionally, this extra data bandwidth has been provided using either special-purpose multiported scalar- and vector-register banks or by using cache memory.

Machines such as the Cray series use special banks of registers to hold operands to feed to the floating-point functional units. Commonly, several individually addressable registers are used to hold scalar quantities. Also, several banks of registers are used to hold vector quantities. Each bank of registers forms a single "vector register," which holds exactly one vector quantity whose length does not exceed the number of registers in a bank.

The advantage of a register-based approach is that it provides quicker access to operands than approaches that simply rely on operands being fetched and stored directly from and to memory. A register-resident value is available in a single clock cycle. A clever compiler can attempt to reuse the register-resident values to reduce the demands on main memory bandwidth, just as registers are used in conventional processors to avoid memory access for operands.

The primary disadvantage of using a register-based approach is that the vector registers are fixed in length and quantity. For example, a given architecture might have 8 vector registers with 32 vector elements each. If some program needed 32 vectors of length 8, the hardware would be unable to provide the needed configuration. This burdens the compiler or an assembly-language programmer with a register-allocation task. Another inflexibility typically found in a vector-register approach is that arbitrary elements in a vector cannot be addressed, nor can operations take place starting at a location other than the first vector element. This can lead to all manner of tricks by the compiler to accomplish seemingly simple operations.

Another disadvantage of a register-based approach is that each register must be multi-ported to allow access by any functional unit. If Titan were to use a pure register-based approach, it would need 6-ported registers to support the six paths into and out of the VDP. Multi-ported registers are very expensive, thus limiting the number of registers available in the final implementation.

Another technique for providing more data bandwidth to the VDP is the use of cache memory, similar to the data-cache memory used on Titan's IPU. Cache memory increases the apparent speed of system memory to the extent that cache hits take place without concerning the compiler with allocating registers.

The disadvantage of using cache is that there is a sharp threshold in the tradeoff between cache size and performance, depending on the size of the arrays being manipulated by the application program. If a program cycles through N elements of memory as a large array before returning to the first element, the cache size must be greater than N elements to avoid flushing the first element fetched before returning to it. For many problems, N is very large and can create the problems illustrated in Example 5.2.

EXAMPLE 5.2.   Effect of array size on cache memory usage.

A significant problem with using data caches for storing arrays is that there is a marked performance degradation once the array size exceeds the available cache memory. For example, let us consider a matrix multiply of two double precision square 2D arrays. The code for a matrix multiply is

```
    DO 100 ROW = 1, N
      DO 200 COL = 1, N
        TEMP = 0.0
        DO 300 INDEX = 1, N
          TEMP = TEMP + LEFT(INDEX,ROW) * RIGHT(COL,INDEX)
300     CONTINUE
        RESULT(COL,ROW) = TEMP
200   CONTINUE
100 CONTINUE
```

where N is the size of the array. If N is 250, each array has 250 × 250 elements, and takes 500,000 bytes each, for a total of 1,000,000 bytes of storage for the arrays LEFT and RIGHT.

Matrix multiplication using the conventional algorithm requires multiplying one row of the first matrix times each column of the second matrix to generate one row of the result. This process is repeated for each row of the first matrix, resulting in

$$2 * N*N \text{ reads / row}$$
$$N \text{ writes / row}$$
$$N * (N + 2*N*N) =$$
$$N**2 + 2*(N**3) \text{ array accesses total}$$

for a matrix multiply, where N is the size of the one side of the matrix. For a 250 × 250 square matrix $N = 250$, and the total number of array accesses is 31,312,500.

If a 1-MB cache is available, the two arrays will just fit into cache completely (assuming that their addresses map into non-overlapping regions of the cache, and that write misses to the cache are not added to the cache). Therefore, each element of the arrays needs to be read only once, and the resulting 250 × 250 array needs to be written once for a total of 187,500 memory accesses. Since a total of 31,312,500 array accesses are required, the cache yields an excellent hit ratio of 99.4%.

But what if the array size were increased to 520 × 520 elements? The total number of array accesses would then be 281,486,400, which is about nine times as many accesses as for the 250 × 250 case, but there is a problem. A 520 × 520 element array takes 2,163,200 bytes, which is more than twice the size of a 1-MB cache. Since the data is more than twice the size of the cache, every element of RIGHT read into the cache for use with the a row of LEFT will be discarded before the next row of LEFT is used (since each element of RIGHT from the first half of the columns in the multiplication pass will be discarded to make room for an array element from the second half of the columns). This gives a 0% hit rate for accesses to the RIGHT array. Assuming that LEFT has a 100% hit ratio after the first access to each element (which is optimistic), the number of accesses to memory for a 520 × 520 array multiply is one read of LEFT, one write of RESULT, and N reads of RIGHT, for a total of 141,148,800 memory accesses. Since a total of 281,486,400 array accesses are required, the cache yields a relatively poor hit ratio of 50.1% and generates 753 times as many memory bus cycles for only nine times as much data as the 250 × 250 case. Actual performance will be even worse, since we have not taken into account the fact that caching of the elements of RIGHT will interfere with rows of LEFT in cache as well.

If a vector register file were used instead of a too-small cache, similar performance results could be obtained for the 520 × 520 case as with using cache. This would require "strip-mining" the multiply so that a partial row of the LEFT matrix was read in, then multiplied against parts of the columns of RIGHT, with the procedure then repeated for remaining portions of the row. This is equivalent to using the vector register file as a software-managed cache for LEFT and not caching RIGHT.

From this example we see that for sufficiently large data sets (where in real applications data sets always tend to be larger than designers anticipate), cache performance is no better than vector register performance. But very large cache memories tend to cost much more in memory chips and control logic than vector registers, while at the same time typically adding a clock cycle or two of latency-to-memory access operations. Thus, the designers of Titan decided to use the VRF instead of a cache for the VPU.

Since there is the potential for such a sharp performance drop with increasing problem size, compilers may be forced to use the same algorithms used in allocating vector registers when accessing memory to avoid flushing the cache with large data structures. This negates the advantages of a programmer-transparent cache; furthermore, large caches must have a slower access time and fewer access ports than small register files for a given level of cost/space/power tradeoff while needing complex control hardware and associative address translation logic for cache management. The result is that, other than providing random access to data elements within a vector, caches do not seem to offer any advantages over vector registers for programs which use large data structures.

The Titan approach to solving the memory bandwidth problem is to use a blend of the best of the vector-register and cache-memory approaches. Titan's VPU has a large Vector Register File (VRF), which is a software-managed cache as shown in Figure 5.8. The VRF is a high-speed memory that holds all data read and written by the VPU. The Titan VPU has a load/store architecture, meaning that all operations execute on data stored in the VRF, and the only references to memory are vector load-and-store instructions between the VRF and system memory.

The VRF contains four banks of 2048 words of 64 bits for storage of vectors and scalars. The VRF is addressed as a small local memory, with no hardware distinction made between vector and scalar quantities; therefore, the VRF may be organized for any combination of scalar and vector quantities at arbitrary boundaries. Accessing of VRF elements as vector quantities is done by specifying a starting VRF address and a length in a vector instruction. The VPU also has limit pointers that allow partitioning the VRF into segments for different tasks, typically a group of 256 ele-

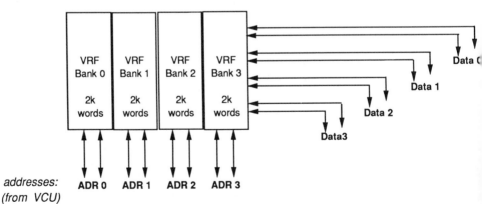

FIGURE 5.8.   The vector register file.

ments from each of the four banks for one task. Each VRF bank is dual-ported with single-cycle access, allowing up to eight simultaneous reads and writes from/to the VRF on each 8 MHz VPU cycle. These features provide Titan with many of the advantages of cache memory, namely flexibility in allocating and addressing vector elements in the register file. Because the VRF is managed by software, complex cache-control logic is eliminated.

Since it is relatively small, the VRF is made of high-speed memory that can be accessed in a single 16 MHz clock. Because it is organized into four banks, each bank need only be dual-ported to provide eight possible access paths. These attributes provide all the advantages of a conventional vector-register arrangement at lower cost than usual. The actual construction of the VRF does not use dual-ported memory chips, since they are expensive and require extra board space. Instead, each of the four banks of the VRF is cycled at a 16 MHz clock rate, allowing two accesses per 8-MHz VPU cycle and giving the effect of a dual-ported 8-MHz register file.

One problem with the VRF design is that the compiler must allocate vectors among the banks to avoid access conflicts. Such an allocation is not always possible, but can be done for most code. When bank conflicts do occur, the conflict is resolved according to a fixed priority, and the remaining bank requestors are stalled to the next memory access cycle.

5.4.3 VECTOR CONTROL UNIT

The VCU, shown in Figure 5.9, contains the control hardware needed to make the rest of the VPU function correctly. The philosophy of the VCU is to provide hardware protection from all possible hazards, as well as automatic hardware detection and exploitation of chaining opportunities.

The VCU contains three vector-address generators for addressing vectors from main memory (two for loading data from the R-BUS and one for storing data via the S-BUS), address generators for the VRF, the interface to the IPU for vector-instruction receipt, and a scoreboard (a hardware control mechanism for maintaining the status of ongoing operations) for chaining and hazard detection.

The vector-address generators are programmed with a base value and stride for accessing vectors in main memory. They provide virtual addresses to the External Translation Lookaside Buffer (ETLB) at up to one address every clock cycle for the store pipe and one address every other clock cycle for the load pipes (which share the RBUS and therefore take turns issuing addresses). The ETLB is actually split into two lookup tables—one for the R-BUS and one for the S-BUS.

The VRF address registers contain a base pointer and a limit pointer for

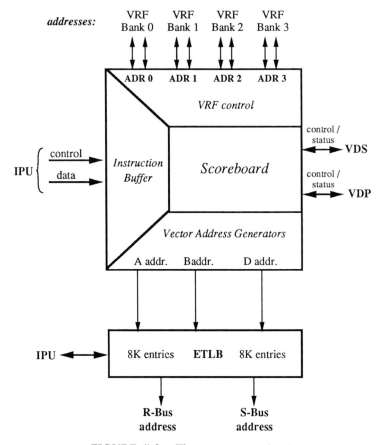

FIGURE 5.9.   The vector control unit.

accessing vectors stored in consecutive locations of the VRF. Because the instruction from the IPU contains enough bits to address the entire VRF, vectors may start and stop at any location within the VRF. The VRF is addressed in such a way that consecutive words lie in the same bank, making it easier for the compiler to place vectors so that they do not cause bank contention.

The scoreboard maintains the status of all instructions that are in execution. It automatically performs chaining if possible and stalls operations that create data hazards. The scoreboard treats scalar instructions as single-element vector instructions to simplify control logic. This has the side effect of allowing multiple scalar instructions to proceed concurrently, with the same hardware hazard and chaining protection afforded to vector operations.

The VCU maintains a seven-deep instruction FIFO (First-In/First-Out) queue from the IPU. The IPU sends vector instructions to the VCU through this FIFO. The VCU accepts as many instructions as possible from the IPU. When an instruction arrives at the VCU that must be delayed due to resource contention, the VCU stalls the IPU (a process that takes six clock cycles to take effect). Since the VCU can accept instructions as fast as the IPU can generate them, anytime the FIFO is non-empty when the IPU issues an instruction, the VCU is considered completely busy. Since the IPU has a peak instruction issue rate of one vector instruction per clock cycle, the IPU may issue up to six additional instructions before the stall condition is detected and acknowledged by the IPU, requiring a seven-element FIFO.

5.4.4 VECTOR DATA SWITCH

The Vector Data Switch connects the eight VRF access paths to the six access paths of the VDP and to the load and store pipes. The VDS, shown in Figure 5.10, routes data among the VRF, the VDP, and the system bus. The VDS is capable of routing up to eight streams of data, which is the maximum number of simultaneous accesses to the VRF allowed. The VDS can route any six of the eight VRF access paths to any of the six VDP data connections simultaneously.

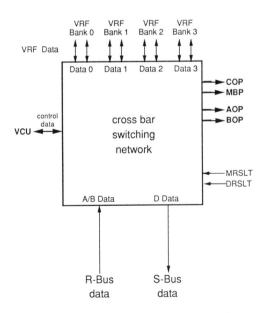

FIGURE 5.10. The vector data switch.

Of course, there must be some way of loading values into and out of the VRF from and to system memory. To accomplish this, the VDS has a single load path shared on alternate cycles between two vector-address generators (A Data and B Data) from memory, allowing two concurrent vector read operations from memory into the VRF. Additionally, the VDS has a single write path and address generator (D Data) to write values to memory. The A and B data paths cannot be active on the same clock cycle, because they share a connection to the RBUS. Therefore, there are eight connections to data sources and sinks outside the VDS: six to the VDP and two to the data bus that may be active simultaneously. This matches the eight paths available to the VRF, removing the VDS as a potential system bottleneck.

An obvious question is why two load paths and only one store path? The answer is that many vector operations are of the form " C ← A op B"; therefore, two loads and a store provide appropriate memory bandwidth to keep the VDP busy.

Because it is very common for vector operations to be fetched from memory and immediately operated upon, the VDS allows fetched operands to be simultaneously stored into the VRF and fed to the VDP for operations. In addition, results can be simultaneously stored into the VRF and written to memory. This mode of operation is called *chaining*. Using chaining, it is possible to have concurrently operating two vector loads to fetch two operand streams, a vector operation, and a vector store to place the result back in memory. If there are no data dependencies, this operation will generate one result every two clock cycles. Another application of chaining is that the output of a VDP operation can be immediately recirculated and fed back to the VDP as the input to another operation. The overall effect of chaining is to reduce the latency between the time that an operand is read from memory or generated as a result from an operation to the time when the result of the operation waiting for the chained operand is completed. Example 5.3 shows how chaining works for a simple operation.

Chaining is implemented in hardware in Titan's Vector Control Unit. If there are data hazards that prevent full-speed chaining or there is a pause for memory access, the VCU will also manipulate the VDS to ensure correct data flow and results.

If all operands needed for a computation are resident in the VRF, the VDP can operate at its full speed of 16 MFLOPS. On the other hand, if all operands needed for a computation are resident in program memory, then chaining will present the operands to the VDP as fast as they can be fetched from memory. The A-Data and B-Data load paths are both connected to the system R-BUS. These two paths operate at a maximum speed of eight million words per second each, which supports the full R-BUS

EXAMPLE 5.3.   Chaining in the VPU.

Chaining occurs when the results of one vector operation are directly used for another operation without waiting for an intermediate storage operation. This allows the second operation to proceed as soon as each element of the first operation is available.

Suppose the following program is being executed:

$$DO \ I = 1, 8$$
$$A(I) = B(I) * C(I)$$
$$CONTINUE.$$

Then, as shown in Figure 5.11, the vectors **B** and **C** would be read from the R-BUS, through the VDS, and then be written into the VRF. If the multiplication operation were not chained, **B** and **C** would subsequently be read from the VRF and routed through the VDP via the VDS, but because the multiplication of **B** and **C** can be chained to the reads of **B** and **C,** the VDS routes the elements of **B** and **C** directly to the VDP as they arrive on the R-BUS.

Similarly, instead of writing the resultant vector **A** to the VRF and then reading the VRF to write **A** to memory, the results from the VDP are chained with the store operation to route elements directly to the S-BUS. Thus, latency for the operation is significantly reduced while preserving correct execution of instructions. Section 5.8 contains an elaboration of this example program showing chaining at an element-by-element level.

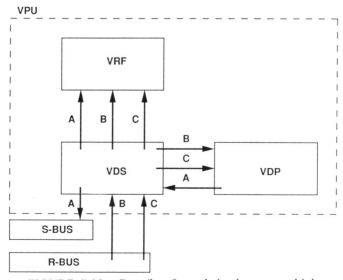

FIGURE 5.11.   Data flow for a chained vector multiply.

bandwidth of 16 MWords/sec, or 128 MBytes/sec. Because two inputs are needed for each floating-point operation, this results in a maximum sustained computation rate of 8 MFLOPS, which is only half the VDP rated maximum. We can now see why vector fetches rate a bus of their own. The R-BUS can easily be saturated by the demands of a single VPU.

The store path operates at a maximum speed of 16 million words per second, so it is not a bottleneck for steady-state operation. Clearly, the extent to which the compiler can allocate values for reuse in the VRF will affect the sustained computation rate of the VDP, as well as the demands the VPU makes on the system bus.

5.4.5   VPU INSTRUCTION SET

All instructions to the VPU come from the IPU through the VPU instruction buffer. The VPU instruction buffer is a memory-mapped device that responds to a certain range of addresses with IPU store commands. Thus, to issue an instruction to the VPU, the IPU first assembles the instruction as data in a register, then performs a store operation of that data to one of the addresses in the VPU instruction buffer address range.

Each VPU instruction consists of a 42-bit value made up of two parts: a 10-bit opcode and a 32-bit operand specifier (Figure 5.12). The 32 bits of the operand specifier are stored by the IPU into the instruction buffer as a 32-bit data element. The 10 bits of the opcode are taken from the lowest 10 bits of the address used by the IPU store operation when accessing the instruction buffer; therefore, the exact address within a 1024-word range at which the IPU stores a VPU instruction determines the opcode, while the 32-bit value that is stored specifies the operand to be used in the computation.

The operand specifier field may have several formats as shown in Figure 5.13. Each format acts as a descriptor of the data to be operated upon, with each opcode requiring a specific operand specifier format.

Each register specifier field in the Scalar operand descriptor format is only five bits wide. This allows reference to a group of 32 registers relative to a frame pointer within the VRF for scalar operations. It is up to the

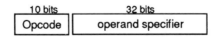

FIGURE 5.12. The VPU instruction format.

Scalar

31	30 16	15 14	10 9	5 4	0
AC <1>	unused	AC <0>	SRx	SRy	SRz

Vector Reduction

31 26	25 21	20 16	15 10	9 5	4 0
unused	VRy <9..5>	VRz <9..5>	unused	VRy <4..0>	VRz<4..0>

Vector Diadic and Triadic

31	30 26	25 21	20 16	15	14 10	9 5	4 0
AC <1>	VRx<9..5>	VRy<9..5>	VRz<9..5>	AC <0>	VRx<0..4>	VRz <0..4>	VRz <0..4>

FIGURE 5.13.   VPU opcode specifier formats.

compiler to manipulate the frame pointer to properly address scalars for a particular procedure. The Accumulator refers to one of the four accumulators built into the VDP.

The Scalar descriptor format is intentionally designed to exploit the IPU's ability to load a 16-bit value as immediate data in a single instruction. In order to generate a scalar instruction, the IPU must execute two MIPS instructions: load a zero-extended, 16-bit immediate value with the operand specifier into a register, then store that register with an offset into the VPU instruction buffer. Since the effective instruction rate of the VPU is 8 MHz and the peak instruction rate of the IPU is 16 MHz, it is possible for the IPU to generate one scalar instruction per VPU instruction cycle for peak performance in certain cases (notably if the instruction refers to accumulator AC0 in the VDP).

The Scalar operand descriptor format can be used to accomplish the scalar operations shown in Table 5.2. In this table, the operation performed by the instruction is listed in the first column. The next three columns contain marks for which operand types are supported by each operation. The possible data types are 64-bit floating-point quantities (F64), 32-bit floating-point quantities (F32), and 32-bit integer quantities (I32). In the operation notation, x, y, and z refer to the registers specified by the three register fields of the descriptor, while AC refers to an accumulator selected by the descriptor field. Some of the type conversion instructions and specialized operations have been omitted for brevity. All operations except division may be performed conditionally (under mask for vector quantities).

TABLE 5.2. Titan scalar operations

Operation	F64	F32	I32
$x = -z$	•	•	
$x = y + z$	•	•	•
$x = y - z$	•	•	•
$x = y \cdot z$	•	•	
$x = y / z$	•	•	
$x = \text{abs}(z)$	•	•	
$x = y \min z$	•	•	•
$x = y \max z$	•	•	•
$x = y \text{ OR } z$			•
$x = y \text{ XOR } z$			•
$x = y \text{ AND } z$			•
$x = \text{NOT } z$			•
$x = AC + z$	•	•	
$x = AC - z$	•	•	
$x = AC \cdot z$	•	•	
$x = AC + y \cdot z$	•	•	
$x = AC - y \cdot z$	•	•	
$x = AC \cdot y + z$	•	•	
$x = AC \cdot y - z$	•	•	
$x = y - AC$	•	•	
$x = z - AC \cdot y$	•	•	
$x = y \cdot z - AC$	•	•	
$AC = y + z$	•	•	
$AC = y - z$	•	•	
$AC = y \cdot z$	•	•	
$AC = y / z$	•	•	
$AC = AC + z$	•	•	
$AC = AC - z$	•	•	
$AC = AC \cdot z$	•	•	
$AC = y - AC$	•	•	

Mask operations use a 256-bit mask vector contained in the VPU's mask register to conditionally perform operations. The contents of the mask vector are set by using a vector comparison instruction. When performing a vector compare, bits in the mask register are set to 1, corresponding to true comparison operations, while false comparison operations set corresponding mask bits to 0. On a masked operation, results are generated only for operands in the vector corresponding to set mask bits. The operations for the masked (i.e., mask bit value of 0) operands are generated, but are not stored in the destination registers or memory locations for the instruction. An example of using a masked operation is to implement a vectorized IF...THEN...ELSE statement to perform different computations on elements of a vector of data which are above and below a certain threshold value.

The Vector Reduction operation-descriptor format is used to specify vectors for use with vector-reduction operations (operations which reduce vector input quantities to accumulated results, as shown in Table 5.3). The starting offset of each of the two vectors is specified, with each offset broken into a high and low field. For example, concatenating bits 20-16 above bits 4-0 would give a 10-bit starting offset value for the z parameter relative to the VRF base pointer. This format is chosen so that a 16-bit immediate data value for the IPU could specify any offsets less than 32. Similarly, any set of vectors which align on 32-word boundaries can be specified with a 16-bit immediate data value as well. In Table 5.3, those quantities which are underlined in the operation column indicate vector quantities, while non-underlined operation elements are scalars. All vector reduction opcodes are available in versions that are unmasked, that use a mask, and that use the bitwise complement of a mask.

The vector length is not specified in the descriptor for any vector operations, but rather is written into a special VPU register which retains the current vector length across multiple operations. This arrangement allows specifying a vector length of up to 256 elements one time for a sequence of loads, operations, and stores.

TABLE 5.3. Titan vector reduction operations.

Operation	F64	F32	I32
$AC = AC + \underline{y} \cdot \underline{z}$	✓	✓	
$AC = AC - \underline{y} \cdot \underline{z}$	✓	✓	
$AC = AC \cdot \underline{y} + \underline{z}$	✓	✓	
$AC = AC \cdot \underline{y} - \underline{z}$	✓	✓	
$AC = \underline{y} \cdot \underline{z} - AC$	✓	✓	
$AC = \underline{y} \cdot \underline{z} - AC$	✓	✓	
$AC = \underline{z} - \underline{y} \cdot AC$	✓	✓	
$AC = \min(\underline{y})$	✓	✓	✓
$AC = \max(\underline{y})$	✓	✓	✓
$AC = OR(\underline{y})$			✓
$AC = AND(\underline{y})$			✓
$AC = XOR(\underline{y})$			✓
$AC = OR(\underline{y})$			✓
$AC = + \underline{y}$	✓	✓	✓
$AC = + \text{abs}(\underline{y})$	✓	✓	
$AC = \max(\text{abs}(\underline{y}))$	✓	✓	

TABLE 5.4.   Titan vector operations.

Operation	F64	F32	I32
$x = -z$	✓	✓	
$x = y + z$	✓	✓	✓
$x = y + z$	✓	✓	✓
$x = y - z$	✓	✓	✓
$x = y - z$	✓	✓	✓
$x = z - y$	✓	✓	✓
$x = y \cdot z$	✓	✓	
$x = y \cdot z$	✓	✓	
$x = \mathrm{abs}(z)$	✓	✓	
$x = y \min z$	✓	✓	✓
$x = y \min z$	✓	✓	✓
$x = y \max z$	✓	✓	✓
$x = y \max z$	✓	✓	✓
$x = \mathrm{NOT}\ z$			✓
$x = y\ \mathrm{OR}\ z$			✓
$x = y\ \mathrm{OR}\ z$			✓
$x = y\ \mathrm{AND}\ z$			✓
$x = y\ \mathrm{AND}\ z$			✓
$x = y\ \mathrm{XOR}\ z$			✓
$x = y\ \mathrm{XOR}\ z$			✓
$x = \mathrm{AC} + z$	✓	✓	
$x = \mathrm{AC} - z$	✓	✓	
$x = \mathrm{AC} \cdot z$	✓	✓	
$x = \mathrm{AC} + y \cdot z$	✓	✓	
$x = \mathrm{AC} - y \cdot z$	✓	✓	
$x = \mathrm{AC} \cdot y + z$	✓	✓	
$x = \mathrm{AC} \cdot y - z$	✓	✓	
$x = y + \mathrm{AC}$	✓	✓	
$x = y - \mathrm{AC}$	✓	✓	
$x = z - \mathrm{AC}$	✓	✓	
$x = y \cdot \mathrm{AC}$	✓	✓	
$x = z - \mathrm{AC} \cdot y$	✓	✓	
$x = y \cdot z - \mathrm{AC}$	✓	✓	

Vector operations are specified using a triple of vector register offsets as shown in Figure 5.13. Table 5.4 summarizes the vector operations that may be performed. As with the Vector Reduction operations, a separate length register is set before the instruction is issued to specify the length of the vector for the operation. As with the Vector Reduction opcodes, all vector Diadic and Triadic opcodes are available in versions that are unmasked, that use a mask, and that use the bitwise complement of a mask.

There are two other instruction types which we shall not delve into in detail. One instruction type is the Compare/Move/Class. This type is used to set mask bits based on the results of comparisons and to conditionally load a vector into vector registers. The other instruction type is used to load constant values into an accumulator, primarily for elementary function evaluation.

5.5 GRAPHICS PROCESSING UNIT

The Graphics Processing Unit (GPU), shown in Figure 5.14, contains the memory for Titan's raster image display as well as special-purpose hardware for accelerating graphics operations. The GPU is physically broken up into two circuit boards. The Graphics Base Board contains the basic system needed to generate images. The Graphics Expansion Board is an option that increases the amount of display memory and rasterizer hardware available.

5.5.1 GRAPHICS CAPABILITIES

Titan keeps all graphics images in dedicated display memory in the GPU. Programs do not directly access graphics memory, but rather build display lists that are interpreted by the special rasterizer hardware units. The rasterizers are capable of drawing points, lines, filled rectangles, and shaded triangles into graphics memory. Peak shaded-triangle drawing with an expansion card is 50 million pixels per second.

A spectrum of tradeoffs between graphics drawing speed and image quality is possible, as shown in Figure 5.15. As one would expect, the higher the image quality, the slower the computation rate.

Titan uses a 1280 horizontal by 1024 vertical pixel raster display. Four graphics display options are available: single-buffered pseudocolor (eight bits per image), double-buffered pseudocolor, single-buffered true color (24 bits per image), and double-buffered true color. All but the double-buffered true-color display may be generated with just the Graphics Base Board.

Single-buffered displays use the same image memory for display and drawing new images. Double-buffered displays use two complete sets of image memory so that one image can be displayed while the next image is drawn with no interference.

The true-color displays use three image memory banks for each buffer, resulting in a picture with eight bits per pixel each for red, green, and blue intensities. This allows 16 million simultaneously displayed colors.

Pseudocolor displays use a single image memory bank to display an entire screen of data, using only eight bits per pixel for color information.

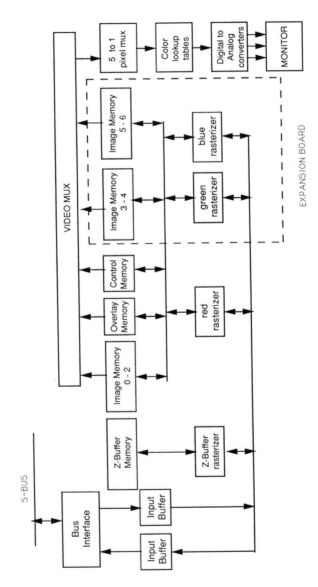

FIGURE 5.14.   The graphics processing unit.

(a)

(b)

(c)

(d)

(e)

FIGURE 5.15. Rendering quality. (a) The Newell teapot, rendered by Doré as a wireframe image. Doré provides a comprehensive range of rendering representations and can switch from one to another without any special coding in the user's application. This image can be rotated and manipulated in real time. (b) Doré can mix rendering representations within one image. Here, the Newell teapot is rendered in wireframe and faceted shading. This image was created from the same data used for the wireframe image, without any recoding in the application. (c) The Newell teapot, represented as a faceted solid. This image can be rotated and manipulated in real time with the Doré toolkit. (d) A smooth-shaded image of the Newell teapot rendered by Doré. This model demonstrates the ability of Doré to provide images with such advanced attributes as reflection. (e) The Newell teapot, rendered in 3D with the Doré integral ray tracer. The Doré toolkit achieves a smooth balance between image realism against computation time. See insert for full-color photo.

The 256 possible values of each eight-bit pixel are used as indices in a color lookup table in the video generation circuitry to select 256 different colors for display. Each of the 256 colors is definable by the user and results in a 24-bit color value being read from the color lookup table.

Each rasterizer is a special-purpose processor that executes instruction streams specifying geometric primitives (primarily lines and triangles) and sets the appropriate bit values in a bank of image memory. For pseudo-color, each image is kept in one bank of image memory on the graphics base board, and the "color rasterizer" manipulates a single bank of memory.

For full-color images, there are two possibilities. If only a graphics base board is available, the three sets of color values (red, green, and blue) are set by the rasterizer one color at a time, using three executions of each geometric primitive with appropriate color-shading parameters for the three colors. If a graphics expansion board is available, each of the three colors for an image is assigned to a different rasterizer, causing the "color rasterizer" to be used as a dedicated "red rasterizer." Since all three rasterizers can work in parallel, drawing rates are sped up by up to a factor of three.

The Z-buffer memory contains 16-bit depth values for each pixel in an image. These depth values are used for hidden surface removal when drawing solid objects. This is accomplished by updating a pixel value with a new value only when the Z attribute of the new pixel is "closer" to the screen than the Z attribute of the existing pixel value. The Z-buffer has its own rasterizer and updates the Z-buffer memory with the depth of the topmost point (the point that is nearest the observer) while objects are being drawn.

There are some graphics-imaging techniques, most notably ray tracing, that are too complicated for the rasterizer hardware components to handle. In these cases, the IPU/VPU perform all the image calculations, then transfer the completed bit map to the image memories using the DMA interface. For less complicated images, the DMA interface fetches instruction streams from display lists resident in system memory.

5.5.2   GPU INSTRUCTION SET

The Graphics Processing Unit takes its instructions from display lists constructed in memory by the IPU. Each display list is a series of GPU instructions which includes commands to draw points, lines, and triangles with various attributes. In this arrangement, the GPU is a processor in its own right, with a special instruction set.

The actual format of the instruction set is quite complicated, with some commands as long as 108 bytes. Table 5.5 contains a summary of the GPU instruction set. Example 5.4 describes a typical instruction format.

TABLE 5.5.   Titan graphics instruction summary.

Operation
Select rasterizers
R/W rasterizer registers
Draw left-facing triangle
Draw right-facing triangle
Draw scan line
Draw vector
Point read
Point write
Read pixel rectangle
Write pixel rectangle
Transfer image rectangle
Block move
Rectangle fill
Read z-buffer rectangle
Write z-buffer rectangle

EXAMPLE 5.4.   An example GPU instruction.

As an example of a GPU instruction, let us examine the format of a scan-line instruction without z-buffering information, as shown in Figure 5.16. The first two words of the instruction contain the opcode and control information. Because each opcode requires a different number of data words, the high half of word zero contains a count field, which is 8 in this case. The 8 refers to the number of data words, exclusive of the first two words of the command.

Since opcode 8 specifies a line-drawing operation, the data words in Figure 5.16 must give information about the endpoints of the line and color information. For this instruction, the machine assumes that the user wishes to draw a line between the screen pixel Cartesian coordinates $(X1,Y1)$ and $(X2,Y2)$. The line is drawn starting at the endpoint with the $(X1,Y1)$ point, where $X1$ must be less than or equal to $X2$. The coordinates of the endpoints are given in the second and third words of the instruction. Each coordinate is given in a fixed-point format specifying a pixel on the screen. This fixed-point format includes an integer portion and a fractional portion. Since endpoints (which are often based upon floating-point values) do not exactly line up with the quantized positions of a pixel, a fixed-point representation allows more accurate placement of the points between the endpoints when the line is drawn.

The last six words of Figure 5.16 specify color information for the line to be drawn. Each pair of words is in the same format and specifies information for one of the three primary colors: Red (words 4 and 5), Green (words 6 and 7), and Blue (words 8 and 9). Let us examine words 4 and 5 as an example pair. Word 4 gives the intensity of the red color for the point (**X**1, **Y**1), again using a fixed-point integer/fraction representation to give better accuracy when drawing the line. Word 5 then gives the change in red intensity per pixel drawn in the line. The Bresenham line-drawing algorithm (Bresenham, 1965) first determines the maximum of the absolute values of (**X**1 − **X**2) and (**Y**1 − **Y**2), then draws one pixel per unit difference of the bigger of the two. Thus, the change in red value per pixel is given in terms of the change per element of the maximum difference in the endpoints.

	31	16	15	4	3	0
word 0	count = 8		0		opcode = 8	

	31	16	15	0
word 1	0		control word	

	31	20	19	16	15	4	3	0
word 2	x1 (INT)		x1 (FRAC)		y1 (INT)		y1 (FRAC)	

	31	20	19	16	15	4	3	0
word 3	x2 (INT)		x2 (FRAC)		y2 (INT)		y2 (FRAC)	

	31	23	15	14	0
word 4	0		Red (INT)	(FRAC)	

	31	23	15	14	0
word 5	0		dRed /dm(INT)	(FRAC)	

	31	23	15	14	0
word 6	0		Green (INT)	(FRAC)	

	31	23	15	14	0
word 7	0		dGreen/dm(INT)	(FRAC)	

	31	23	15	14	0
word 8	0		Blue(INT)	(FRAC)	

	31	23	15	14	0
word 9	0		dBlue/dm(INT)	(FRAC)	

FIGURE 5.16. Scan-line instruction format.

5.5.3   GRAPHICS PIPELINE

The graphics support hardware is very general in nature, consisting of simple point, line-, and triangle-drawing hardware in the GPU and general-purpose processing in the CPU. This use of general-purpose hardware was intentional to avoid the problem of designing specific graphics hardware for a particular rendering algorithm, only to have the hardware made obsolete by the discovery of a superior algorithm. By using general-purpose hardware, Titan not only can keep its graphics display algorithms up-to-date, but can also allow a choice of speed vs level of detail when drawing objects.

Because of this design philosophy, it is appropriate to talk about the graphics software pipeline. This software pipeline is a series of steps used to compute pixel values when given a description of a set of objects in a three-dimensional coordinate space. It is not an actual piece of hardware, but may be thought of as a virtual hardware graphics-display system that is built of the various Titan components and controlled by graphics software. Figure 5.17 shows the 10 steps of the graphics software pipeline. The pipeline uses a mixture of CPU and GPU resources to render images.

The overall organization of the graphics pipeline is a sequential set of steps proceeding from an object list to pixel values. Since Titan is a vector machine with a finite-size vector-register file, it is advantageous to break an object list into groups. Thus, most of the pipeline is repeated in a loop, with a batch of 16 or 32 objects processed on each pass of the loop. The overall goal of the graphics code organization is to keep as many values as possible in registers, and in particular in the VRF. In order to accomplish its task with high efficiency, the graphics pipeline uses all 8192 vector registers available in the VRF.

A second objective of the graphics pipeline is to prune non-visible objects as soon as possible; furthermore, the operations are arranged so that this early pruning is accomplished before any computationally expensive operations have been performed. This means that the last few stages of the pipeline are the most expensive computationally, but at the same time they process the fewest possible objects (ideally, only those objects that actually appear on the screen). With three-dimensional solid modeling, there are often a large number of hidden objects, so this strategy produces important speedups.

The first stage of the pipeline is a three-dimensional transformation that is applied only to mesh-data structures (sets of objects supplied in a mesh-connected array). In this process, the mesh data is converted into an explicit list of objects required by later phases. The second stage of the pipeline is a trivial rejection clipping stage, in which objects which will

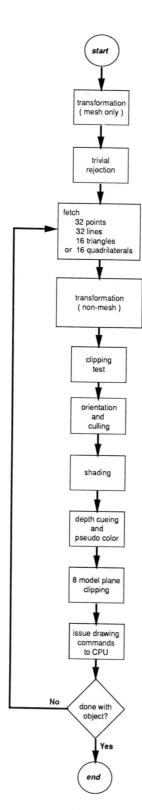

FIGURE 5.17.
Graphics software
pipeline.

obviously not be visible on the screen (because they are too far from the field of view) are pruned from the display list.

The third stage begins the iterated portion of the graphics pipeline. Here 32 points, 32 lines, 16 triangles, or 16 quadrilaterals are batched together as a set of vector registers for processing. The fourth through ninth stages of the pipeline perform conventional three-dimensional object rendering, including clipping, orientation, culling (hidden polygon removal), shading, depth cueing (varying shading to make objects "further" from the viewer slightly darker), pseudocoloring, and model plane clipping.

Up until this point, all stages have been processed by the CPU. The IPU has been used for control information, while the VPU has been used to process the vectors of data structures. In the tenth pipeline stage, the IPU builds a command list in memory, then starts the GPU processing the command list. While the GPU is drawing the objects, the CPU begins another pass through the graphics pipeline. In this manner, the CPU and GPU work are overlapped at a reasonably fine grain while drawing objects.

5.6   I/O

As with any computer, Titan needs input and output in order to execute real programs. Graphics display is considered such an important output device that it merited its own section. This section deals with the other I/O devices used to store programs and data. Figure 5.18 shows the I/O subsystem components.

5.6.1   THE I/O BUS

The I/O bus is used primarily for disk storage and for communication with other high-speed devices. The I/O bus supports two SCSI channels, each of which can sustain a transfer rate of 4 MB/sec. The hard disks used in Titan can sustain a transfer rate of 1 MB/sec, and up to eight disk drives may be connected to each of the SCSI channels.

The other high-speed connection to the I/O bus is a VME bus adapter. This allows Titan to communicate at high speeds with other processors, perhaps for data capture, and to use mass storage devices compatible with the VME bus. The VME bus provides a 15 MB/sec transfer rate.

5.6.2   THE MICRO BUS

The micro bus is loosely based on the Intel 8086 chip's bus scheme as popularized by the IBM PC computer series. The micro bus is driven by

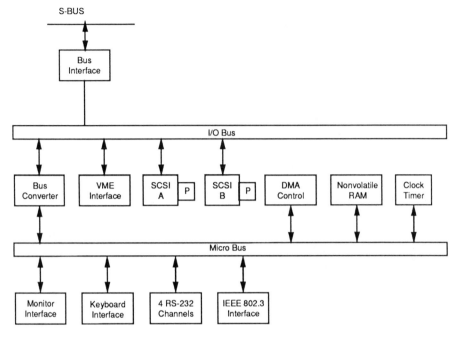

FIGURE 5.18. The I/O subsystem.

an I/O Bus/Micro Bus converter and is capable of transfer rates of 2 MB/ sec. Among the resources connected to the Micro Bus are the keyboard and mouse interface, the sound generator, the system time-of-day clock, nonvolatile RAM for storing configuration information, and interfaces to slow external device buses.

5.7   RELIABILITY FEATURES

While often an afterthought in designing a computer, features to improve reliability are vital in a high-performance machine. Getting a fast answer to a question is not acceptable if each time the program is run the answer is different (and wrong)! In Titan, great care was taken during the design process to install mechanisms to increase the reliability of the system and provide for detection and/or correction of errors that may occur.

Figure 5.19 shows the error checking and correcting features of Titan.

In the figure, P stands for parity bit and ECC stands for error-correcting code bits in the data paths. G stands for a parity-generating device, C stands for a parity-checking device, and CRC stands for a cyclic redundancy-check device.

5.7.1   MEMORY SUBSYSTEM ERROR CORRECTION

Since high-density DRAM chips are subject to soft errors from alpha particles (which can disrupt the energy stored in a bit of memory, causing data loss), Titan's memory subsystem has Single Error Correction, Multiple Error Detection (SECMED) error checking and correction logic. The SECMED scheme used allows hardware correction of any single bit error, and detection of any 2 bit errors, as well as any 3- or 4-bit errors within a single chip. Since 4-bit wide DRAM chips are used, the detection of multiple errors within a single chip is important to handle a faulty chip. A memory-scrubbing operation is provided to correct single-bit errors before a second soft error can occur.

5.7.2   SYSTEM BUS ERROR PROTECTION

The Titan bus, which forms the backbone of the system, is extensively protected by parity including:

- Parity on control signals including cycle type, access type, read, write, and spare (1 bit)
- Byte parity on address (4 bits),
- Parity on request number (1 bit),
- Byte parity on data (8 bits), and
- Parity on return ID (1 bit).

Errors can be forced on the address, data, and some control fields (i.e., cycle type and access type) by inverting the sense of a bit. Other errors detected by the bus include

- Non-existent address,
- Bus time out,
- Invalid transaction type, and
- Address alignment error.

The sender at the time of an error is recorded to assist isolation to the field replaceable unit.

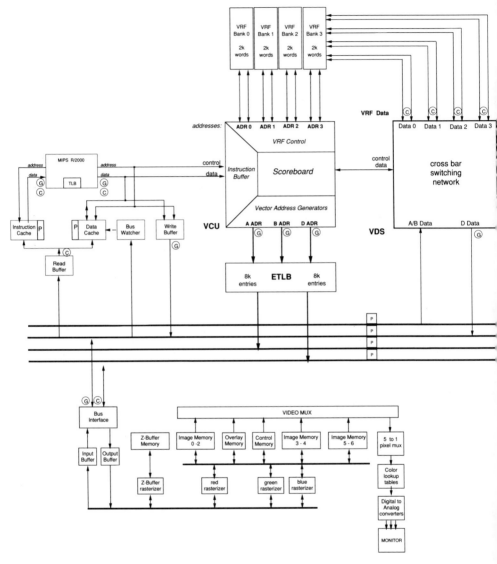

FIGURE 5.19. Error checking and correction in Titan.

146

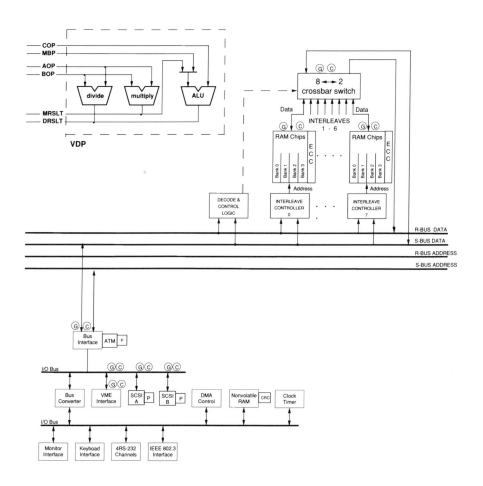

5.7.3 OTHER PROTECTION AND DIAGNOSTIC MECHANISMS

For a very reliable system, every element of storage should have some sort of protection mechanism (parity or error correction). The longer data is likely to reside in a memory bit, the more important it is for the bit to be protected in some manner, because the probability of a soft error rises with time. Some of the additional protection in Titan includes:

· Parity on the I/O Address Translation Map prevents writing to memory at a location pointed to by a corrupted address, and

· Byte parity on the data and instruction caches of the IPU.

As an additional aid, the diagnostic port is closely coupled with the IPU and boot ROM. Thus only a small portion of the machine needs to be working in order for remote assistance to be available.

5.8   AN EXAMPLE OF SYSTEM OPERATION

Now that we have examined the operation of each component of the system, let us look at a large-scale example of how the different system components tie together. This is an elaboration of Example 5.3. The example we shall use will be a simple vector multiply:

```
DO I = 1, 8
    A(I) = B(I) * C(I)
CONTINUE
```

The purpose of this example is to show the flow of instructions and data throughout the system. Figure 5.11 shows the flow of data within the VPU. Figure 5.20 is a table which shows all the major system resources along with which pieces of data are manipulated for each clock period of our example (some simplifications have been made).

The code will be executed by first loading the elements of B( ) using vector load pipe *a*, loading the elements of C( ) using vector load pipe *b*, performing a vector multiply to form the result A( ) in a vector register, then storing the vector register values of A( ) to memory. Titan assembly code for this would be of the form

```
dvlda R0, B       | Double precision vector load, pipe a
dvldb R1, C       | Double precision vector load, pipe b
dvmul R2, R0, R1  | Double precision vector multiply
dvst R2, A        | Double precision vector store.
```

For purposes of clarity, we are ignoring the instructions needed to set the length of the vector operations and other details. We shall also assume that there are no system stalls during execution (i.e., no cache misses, no VRF bank conflicts, no memory interleave conflicts, no system bus conflicts, etc.). The clock column shows the number of 16 MHz clock cycles for this multiply.

The IPU column shows that it takes three MIPS R2000 clock cycles to build and submit the dvlda instruction to the VPU instruction queue, and three more each for dvldb, dvmul, and dvst. Once the dvst instruction is issued, the IPU is free to perform other computations, including the submission of other vector unit instructions.

The Vector Control Unit takes two clock cycles to set up scoreboard entries for each instruction issued by the IPU. Once the scoreboard entries have been put in place, memory fetches for the operands proceed using the R-BUS. Note how the fetches for the C( ) operands are interleaved with those for the B( ) operands by using both the a and b load pipes. The DATA entries for the R-BUS column show when data is read back from memory.

The MEMORY column shows the clock cycles used to read a memory address from the R-BUS and return the data to the R-BUS. At the bottom of the MEMORY column, we see the resultant A( ) vector elements written into memory from the S-BUS, even as the final elements of C( ) are being read from memory. The latency for actually storing the results from the S-BUS into memory is not shown, since it does not affect further operations in the VPU.

The VDS column shows that as elements are read in from memory, they spend a clock cycle in the VDS awaiting transfer to the VRF (since the dvlda and dvldb instructions load operands into the VRF). When the C(1) element is read in, the scoreboard recognizes the fact that it already has the B(1) element available, and immediately routes both C(1) and B(1) to the VDP at the same time as the VRF is written with C(1). This is an example of chaining, where the multiply is started by the VDP as soon as the two loads have progressed far enough to provide appropriate operands.

After a six-clock cycle latency from the time operands are available to the VDP, the VDP produces the elements of the A( ) vector, which are routed through the VDS and into the VRF. In another instance of chaining, the VDS also writes the elements of A( ) to memory using the S-BUS as soon as they are available.

From the clock column, we can see that the latency of the code sequence is 40 clock cycles for eight multiplies; however, this execution rate of 3.2 MFLOPS is pessimistic, since all of the system resources are idle for portions of this example and could be productively used for other operations

CLK	IPU	VCU	RBUS ADDR	RBUS DATA	SBUS ADDR	SBUS DATA	MEMORY ADDR	MEMORY DATA	VDS	VRF	VDP
0	–										
1	–										
2	dvlda										
3	–	dvlda									
4	–	dvlda									
5	dvldb		B (1)				B (1)				
6	–	dvldb	B (2)				B (2)				
7	–	dvldb	C (1)				C (1)				
8	dvmul		B (3)				B (3)				
9	–	dvmul	C (2)				C (2)				
10	–	dvmul	B (4)				B (4)				
11	dvst		C (3)				C (3)	B (1)			
12		dvst	B (5)	B (1)			B (5)	B (2)	B (1)		
13		dvst	C (4)	B (2)			C (4)	C (1)	B (2)	B (1)	
14			B (6)	C (1)			B (6)	B (3)	C (1)	B (2)	
15			C (5)	B (3)			C (5)	C (2)	B (3)	C (1)	
16			B (7)	C (2)			B (7)	B (4)	C (2)	B (3)	
17			C (6)	B (4)			C (6)	C (3)	B (4)	C (2)	
18			B (8)	C (3)				B (5)	C (3)	B (4)	B (1) C (1)
19											B (2) C (2)

Row									
20	C (7)	B (5)		C (4)	B (8)		B (5)	C (3)	B (3) C (3)
21	C (8)	C (4)	A (1)	B (6)	C (7)		C (4)	B (5)	B (4) C (4) A (1)
22		B (6)	A (2)	C (5)	C (8)	A (1)	B (6)	C (4)	B (5) C (5) A (2)
23		C (5)	A (3)	B (7)		A (2)	C (5)	B (6)	B (6) C (6) A (3)
24		B (7)	A (4)	C (6)	B (7)	A (3)	B (7)	C (5)	B (7) C (7) A (4)
25		C (6)	A (5)	B (8)	C (6)	A (4)	C (6)	B (7)	B (8) C (8) A (5)
26		B (8)	A (6)	C (7)	B (8)	A (5)	B (8)	C (6)	A (6)
27		C (7)	A (7)		C (7)	A (6)	C (7)	B (8)	A (7)
28			A (8)	C (8)		A (7)		C (7)	A (8)
29		C (8)			C (8)	A (8)	C (8)		
30				A (4)			A (4)	A (3)	A (5)
31				A (5)			A (5)		A (6)
32				A (6)		A (5)	A (6)		
33				A (6)		A (5)			A (7)
34				A (7)		A (6)	A (6)		
35				A (7)		A (6)			A (8)
36				A (8)		A (7)	A (7)		
37				A (8)		A (7)			
38				A (8)		A (8)	A (8)		
39				A (8)		A (8)			

FIGURE 5.20. Example of system operation.

TABLE 5.6.   Titan feature summary.

	Intrainstruction	Interinstruction	Control Method
Buffering			
VPU instruction buffer		•	HW
IPU write buffer		•	HW
VRF		•	HW
VRF		•	SW
TLB and ETLB		•	HW/SW
Cache		•	HW
GPU frame buffer		•	HW/SW
Pipelining			
Bus	•	•	SW
Memory interleaves	•	•	HW
VPU	•	•	HW
VDP	•	•	HW
Concurrency			
Bus	•	•	HW/SW
IPU, VPU		•	HW/SW
CPUs		•	SW
CPU, GPU, I/O		•	SW
VDP	•	•	HW/SW
VRF	•	•	HW/SW
I/O devices		•	HW

during the idle time. For instance, the VDP is only in use between clocks 16 and 31, since other inputs could be fed into the VDP pipeline during other clocks; furthermore, since only the multiplier is in use, it is possible that a vector addition could proceed in parallel with this example at any time.

5.9   FEATURE SUMMARY

In this chapter, we have talked about several system areas which have varying degrees of overlap and concurrence. Table 5.6 is a summary of those features in Titan. The three major categories for overlap and concurrence are buffering, pipelining, and concurrency through replication. The table shows how these three areas are incorporated into the Titan design, along with whether they are intra-instruction or inter-instruction features, and whether they are implemented in hardware or software.

CHAPTER
S I X

ARCHITECTURAL
ANALYSIS OF
TITAN

Now that we have seen the details of Titan's construction, we can estimate the performance to be expected from the system. The basic approach used in this chapter is to do capacity analysis (data flow rates, computation rates, and the like) to see where any bottlenecks might be. From this, we can estimate the maximum system performance possible. At the same time, we can determine the balance of the Titan architecture.

6.1   SYSTEM BUS

The system bus consists of two components: the S-BUS and the R-BUS. By using the split transaction protocol on this synchronous bus, Titan is able to sustain a rate of one bus transaction per clock cycle on each of the two buses. Since each bus is 64 bits wide, the maximum available bandwidth is

$$(2 \text{ buses} * 8 \text{ Bytes}) / 62.5 \text{ ns per word}$$
$$= 256 \text{ MB/sec for the system.}$$

6.2   MEMORY

The three levels of memory in Titan all have different levels of performance. We shall examine each in turn.

153

6.2.1 CACHE MEMORY

The IPU's caches provide instructions and data to the MIPS R2000 processor. A cache read miss for either the I-cache or the D-cache results in a bus cycle to memory to fetch the needed data. This results in a pause of about 17 cycles to fetch the 64-bit word, depending on exactly how the miss occurs. Figure 6.1 shows how the clock cycles for a typical cache miss are expended. This high latency is caused by the protocol that is implemented to give good throughput on a shared bus as well as the many layers of circuitry between the processor and memory.

A 17-clock cycle wait for data is a very expensive penalty on a processor that strives for one-clock cycle per instruction, so IPU performance is heavily dependent on the cache hit ratio. Unfortunately, cache hit ratios depend heavily on the application program being executed. The cache hit ratio for Titan often ranges from 80% to 100%, depending on the software being executed. Figure 6.2 shows the relationship between the hit ratio and the instructions executed per second, assuming that all instructions execute in a single clock cycle when they get a cache hit. From this diagram, we can see that performance is severely affected by even a small number of misses, with a miss rate of just 5% cutting performance by

Clock	Action
0	look up in cache
1	recognize cache miss, stall processor
2	generate address for bus read
3	generate address for bus read
4	generate address for bus read
5	arbitrate for bus
6	arbitrate for bus
7	assert address on bus
8	memory interleave access
9	memory interleave access
10	memory interleave access
11	memory interleave access
12	read data from bus (low word)
13	read data from bus (high word)
14	send data to IPU
15	cache miss fix-up cycle on IPU
16	restart IPU

FIGURE 6.1. IPU cache miss.

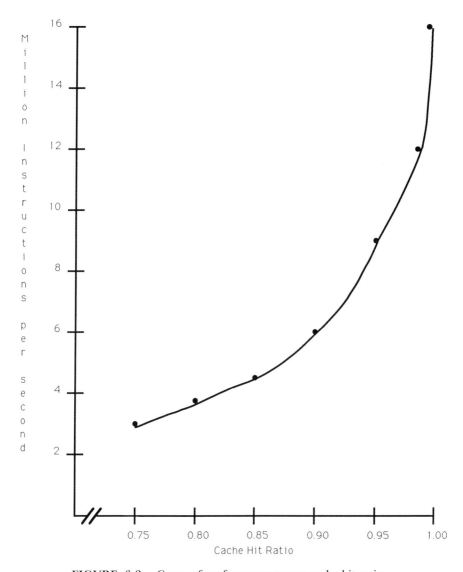

FIGURE 6.2. Curve of performance versus cache hit ratio.

nearly 50%. Fortunately, the actual speed of the IPU is usually not a limitation on Titan when running scientific code, since scientific-code execution time is dominated by floating-point vector computations. The actual memory traffic generated by IPU cache misses will be calculated in the section on IPU performance.

6.2.2   PHYSICAL MEMORY

The fact that Titan supports eight or 16 interleaves of memory greatly increases the available memory bandwidth. The total cycle time of the memory is six clock cycles per access; therefore, the memory bandwidth available from each interleave is

$$8 \text{ bytes } / \, (\, 6 \text{ cycles} * 62.5 \text{ ns }) \, = \, 21.5 \text{ MB/sec}$$

The total available bandwidth depends on the number of interleaves available. For an eight-way interleaved system, this gives a bandwidth of 172 MB/sec. For a 16-way interleaved system, the available bandwidth is 344 MB/sec.

Since the system bus is limited to a total of 256 MB/sec, an eight-way interleaved system is clearly memory limited. A 16-way interleaved system appears at first glance to have excess memory bandwidth. However, to the extent that memory accesses are not well-behaved with respect to uniform access to interleaves over time, memory response time is degraded. The addition of the extra memory interleaves and accompanying excess bandwidth reduces the occurrence of conflicts and thus offsets to some extent the inherent inefficiencies in using interleaves in the real world.

The Titan architecture is optimized for vectorized floating-point operations, which are well suited to an interleaved memory access scheme. For future discussions, we will assume that the 16-way interleaved system is used, since this interleave factor can be arranged for any Titan system with two memory boards installed. We shall also assume that the access patterns of the software allow the full 256 MB/sec access rate supported by the system bus, which is a reasonable assumption for many scientific programs.

6.2.3   VIRTUAL MEMORY

A TLB miss on the IPU takes approximately 800 nanoseconds to process in the likely case that the handling routine is resident in the IPU instruction cache. This may slow down considerably if the handling routine has been flushed from cache or if the page addressed has been migrated from physical memory to disk.

The VPU uses an External Translation Lookaside Buffer (ETLB) to map all vector addresses into physical memory addresses. Whenever an ETLB miss is detected, the IPU is interrupted and performs the necessary service to load the appropriate entry into the ETLB. Servicing an ETLB miss takes from 25 microseconds to 300 microseconds, depending on the number of instruction cache misses encountered by the IPU when processing the ETLB miss.

The impact of virtual memory on system performance depends on a large number of factors such as installed physical memory size, number of tasks being executed, memory requirements of each task, and the memory access patterns of each task. In a time-shared system these effects can become very important; however, for measuring the speedup on the machine for a single task, the impact of virtual memory is usually quite small. In the analysis of Titan, we shall assume that there is enough physical memory installed to run the given task and ignore the effects of virtual memory overhead.

6.3   INTEGER UNIT

The number of instructions that the IPU may execute per second depends on both available memory bandwidth and on the internal design of the R2000. Data dependencies affect the pipeline in the R2000 by requiring no-ops that form pipeline "bubbles." These bubbles are required when results of computations are needed as inputs for later computations before the results are ready and when the branch delay slot after a conditional branch cannot be filled with a useful instruction. The impact of these inefficiencies is strongly dependent on the program being executed and the cleverness of the high-level language compiler.

The primary limit to execution speed for the IPU is the number of cache misses. On a cache hit, the result being read from memory is returned without pausing the processor. On a cache miss, 17 clock cycles pass before the 64-bit word containing the data or instruction is available, stalling the IPU. The number of instructions that may be executed per second by the IPU is

16 MHz / (hit ratio + (miss penalty*(1 − hit ratio))) =

instructions per second.

In Titan, the miss penalty is 17 clock cycles, so the formula is

16 MHz / (hit ratio + (17 * (1 − hit ratio))) =

instructions per second.

The cache hit ratio also controls the amount of memory bus bandwidth used by the IPU. Every successful access to cache memory avoids the need for an access to system memory over the system bus. The amount of bus bandwidth used by the IPU is given by the formula

(Instructions per second) * (1 − hit ratio) =

bus bandwidth in words per second.

Reducing this, and taking into account that there are 8 bytes in each bus word, the bus bandwidth taken by the IPU is

$$\frac{128 * (1 - \text{hit})}{17 - (16 * \text{hit})} = \text{bus bandwidth in MB/sec}$$

Just to get some feel for the numbers involved, let's assume a 95% cache hit ratio. The IPU performance would be 8.89 million instructions per second, with a required bus bandwidth of 3.56 MB/sec. We shall ignore the effects of TLB misses for this calculation, since they will have minimal impact on bus bandwidth requirements.

There is no correct answer to how fast the IPU must be by itself. Performance of the IPU must be sufficiently fast to avoid keeping other system resources waiting for it to perform control functions.

6.4   VECTOR PROCESSING UNIT

The maximum bandwidth provided by the VRF is 64 MWords/sec = 512 MB/sec. Contention for use of more than two data elements at a time from a single bank can reduce the bandwidth available to a program. Fortunately, compilers can schedule which data are assigned to each bank to minimize conflicts.

The primary product of the VPU is floating-point computations. The VPU uses multiple specialized hardware units as well as pipelining at many levels to increase execution speed. To get an approximation of the VPU computation power, we will ignore all operations except floating-point multiplication and floating-point addition.

The multiplier and ALU are each able to produce eight million results per second, for an aggregate processing rate of 16 MFLOPS. Since each operation takes two inputs and produces one output, this requires 48 MWords, or 384 MB/sec, of data transfer rate for full-speed operation. This 384 MB/sec data rate exceeds the 256 MB/sec system bus transfer rate, so the VPU is limited by the extent to which VRF elements can be reused in computations.

The VRF must have enough capacity to handle not only the 384 MB/sec computation data flow rate, but also simultaneous loads and stores to and from program memory. The VDP supports a data flow rate of 128 MB/sec from the R-BUS, and a peak data flow rate of 128 MB/sec to the S-BUS (although only an average rate of 64 MB/sec is realistically necessary as discussed in Chapter 5). Thus, the total bandwidth demand on the VRF is

$$384 + 128 + 128 = 640 \text{ MB/sec.}$$

This does not fit within the 512 MB/sec capacity of the VRF, so there at first appears to be a bandwidth problem for the VRF. But perhaps we have been too demanding in our bandwidth calculations.

In computing a 384-MB/sec bandwidth for the VDP, we assumed that the multiplier and adder were working independently; however, the crucial code sequences for vector machine performance tend to be operations which reuse the multiplier output as one of the operands to the adder (we will discuss this operation, called DAXPY, in Chapter 7). For this case, only three inputs are needed to the VDP, resulting in a 256-MB/sec demand from the VDP, and a 512-MB/sec demand to and from the VRF, which exactly matches the available VRF bandwidth. To the extent that the compiler is unsuccessful in scheduling VRF accesses across banks to avoid bank conflict, the VRF available bandwidth is degraded below the potential 512 MB/sec and performance suffers.

6.4.1 VECTOR VERSUS SCALAR PERFORMANCE

There is a tradeoff in vector processors between the overhead associated with the initiation of a vector instruction and the speed with which steady-state vector operations occur. Scalar computations can be specified by a single IPU instruction that feeds a command to the VCU. Vector computations require a more complicated specification but result in a higher steady-state execution rate (one result every second clock cycle) once the process is started. It may be that for short vectors a sequence of scalar operations can be done faster than a single vector instruction with all of its associated setup overhead. In general, there is a crossover vector length below which scalar computations are faster and above which vector computations are faster.

Titan has a vector/scalar crossover length of two. Because of implementation details in the R2000 IPU, the VCU recognizes a special 16-bit format floating-point instruction as a scalar instruction (vector with implicit length of one), which can be generated in a single clock cycle by the R2000. Vector instructions take a 32-bit value to specify both a VRF starting location and a length. Thirty-two-bit values can be generated by the R2000 in two clock cycles, allowing a vector command of length two to be generated by the IPU in the same amount of time as two scalar VPU commands (assuming other overhead operations such as changing the contents of the vector length register are not required).

Another issue in vector machine design is that of latency in executing instructions. Sometimes successive vector instructions cannot be executed concurrently because of data dependencies. In this case, the total time taken for a vector instruction matters. Since the total execution time is a combination of instruction setup latency and actual execution time, longer vectors perform better than shorter vectors. The instruction setup latency is related to pipeline latencies in Titan from the time the VCU generates a VRF address for the first operand until that operand reaches the VDP and the time between the last result leaves the VDP and that result is written into the VRF.

6.5   GRAPHICS PROCESSING UNIT

In system operation, the IPU may be considered a control unit for the GPU. When drawing simple images, the IPU is responsible for setting up a display list in program memory, then initiating GPU execution of that display list. For more complicated images, the IPU uses the VPU to perform geometric calculations, then uses the results of those computations to build a display list for the GPU. In both cases, there can be concurrency between the display list generation and execution of previously formed display lists by the GPU.

Since triangles are used to draw most three-dimensional objects on Titan, we shall examine triangle-drawing rates when determining the demands the GPU places upon the rest of the system.

Each full-color triangle requires 112 bytes of display list memory to be interpreted by the GPU. Full-color triangles can be generated at 18.9 million pixels per second with an expanded GPU for 400-pixel triangles. This works out to 47,250 triangles per second, which is a load of 5.3 MB/sec on the system bus.

When complex image generation techniques such as ray tracing are used, however, the situation changes. Each full-color image takes 3.9 MBytes of memory, which must be DMAed into the graphics buffers. Since this image must have been written by a processor into main memory, actually 7.8 MBytes of system-bus bandwidth are used in just writing an image and displaying it. At a minimal update rate of five frames per second for limited animation, this results in 39.0 MB/sec bus loading just for transferring the image data, which is almost one-third of the available S-BUS bandwidth. Of course, techniques such as ray tracing which require buffer transfers are usually too computationally demanding, and therefore too slow, to make animation practical, so this high transfer rate is not seen in practice.

6.6   I/O

The I/O subsystem has several communications channels that may be used to move data in and out of memory in parallel with other computations.

The I/O subsystem can load the S-BUS with 8 MB/sec of activity from the disk drives. We shall not worry about the Micro Bus or the VME bus for this analysis.

6.7 ANALYSIS OF SYSTEM THROUGHPUT AND PLUMBING DIAGRAM

Now that we have examined Titan's subsystems, let us look at a data transfer "plumbing diagram" of the machine. The idea is to see if the machine's data transfer rates are well balanced and to find limits to processing speed based on data flow rate. Figure 6.3 shows the diagram we shall be discussing. Please note that this diagram does not exactly show the hardware in the way it is built, but rather is rearranged to help in understanding the way data moves in the system. In particular, the VRF of the VPU is shown between the vector unit and the buses, since the purpose of the VRF is to act as a software-managed cache to reduce memory bus traffic.

We know that the S-BUS and R-BUS can supply 128 MB/sec of bandwidth each. If the memory is 16-way interleaved, it can supply the total 256 MB/sec usable by the buses within the limits of interleave bank conflicts, so we shall say that Titan has 128 MB/sec of bandwidth available on each bus.

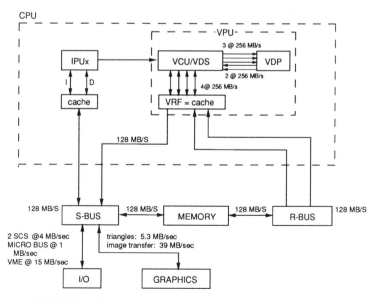

FIGURE 6.3. Conceptual "plumbing" diagram of Titan.

6.7.1   THE S-BUS

First, let us look at the S-BUS in more detail. The S-BUS is the general-purpose system bus that serves everything except the VPU input pipes. The heaviest consumer of the S-BUS is the VPU, which uses the S-BUS to store its results into memory.

If the VPU is executing a single vector operation at 8 MFLOPS, the VPU will generate only 64 MB/sec of the possible 128 MB/sec transfer rate from the store pipe. The extra capacity of the store pipe can be used to "catch up" when other factors have tied up the S-BUS during a vector operation. Because of reasoning that will be explained in the following section on the R-BUS, we can assume that each VPU will generate only half of the 64 MB/sec traffic, resulting in a two-VPU load of 64 MB/sec on the S-BUS.

After the VPUs, the IPUs are the next heaviest users of memory bandwidth. The memory traffic generated by the IPUs depends heavily on the cache hit rate, which is extremely software-dependent. We shall estimate a 95% hit rate on both the I-cache and D-cache of the IPU. If we assume that one in two instructions accesses the D-cache, this leads to a cache miss approximately once every 13 clock cycles. Each cache miss causes the processor to pause for 17 clock cycles, resulting in one memory transaction every 30 clock cycles, for a bus bandwidth of 4.2 MB/sec per IPU. If two IPUs are installed, this is a total bus demand of 8.4 MB/sec.

The I/O subsystem can load the S-BUS with 8 MB/sec of activity from the disk drives. After the I/O bus comes the graphics interface. If triangles are being drawn into a full color image buffer, the rasterizers need 5.3 MB/sec of memory bandwidth for fetching display lists, so we have a total of

$$64 + 8.4 + 8 + 5.3 = 85.7 \text{ MB/sec}$$

demand on the S-BUS, which means that the S-BUS has plenty of excess capacity for the case analyzed.

There is another case of interest. If graphics of higher quality than can be generated by the GPU's rasterizers are desired, images must be built in program memory and transferred to the graphics buffer. This increases the demand upon the S-BUS from 5.3 MB/sec to 39 MB/sec for a five-frame-per-second update rate. This extra demand increases the S-BUS traffic to 119.4 MB/sec, still within the S-BUS capacity.

So it seems that the S-BUS has more capacity than is needed. This extra capacity is well-spent, however, since the effects of bursts of cache misses from the IPU when changing context and bursts of I/O transfers from the VME bus can easily soak up the extra memory bandwidth for short periods of time.

6.7.2 THE R-BUS

The R-BUS exists only to provide data to the vector units. A vector unit performing a single chained vector operation of the form LOAD—LOAD—OP—STORE (for example, a vector add) can execute at a rate of 8 MFLOPS, requiring two inputs for each operation. This requires a data fetching rate on the bus of 64 MB/sec for each input, or a total of 128 MB/sec. Thus, even a single vector operation can saturate the R-BUS.

Fortunately, some vector operations are able to use results already resident in the VRF. Additionally, there are latencies associated with sequences of small vectors, and the VPU will be idle at times while the program is executing integer-oriented code. It is reasonable to estimate that these effects will combine to cut the required bus bandwidth in half for each vector unit. We therefore come to the conclusion that Titan is bus limited by the R-BUS when it has two or more vector units installed.

Of course, this analysis is only for single vector operations. It is possible to have simultaneous vector multiplications and additions running at a total rate of 16 MFLOPS. If all operands come from memory, this would, of course, completely swamp the R-BUS. Fortunately, a very common purpose for doing simultaneous multiplies and additions is for matrix multiplication, which simply recirculates a running sum to accumulate the inner product. In this case, only two operands per multiply/add pair are required from memory, which does not increase the bandwidth requirements of the computation beyond that of a single vector operation. This would still suggest that a two-processor Titan would usually swamp the bus; however, much of the time of a computation is spent performing other operations that are not able to use the capacity of the VPU fully or are able to reuse data located in the VRF. In these cases, more than two processors can be supported by the bus with increased overall computation speed.

There is a special case of numeric-intensive code that is executed on Titan: graphics transformations. Graphics transformations require many computations on a small amount of data. For this reason, it is possible that a third vector unit may be added to Titan for processing graphics transformations while still having only modest restrictions due to bus bandwidth limitations, so what may make sense from a "plumbing" point of view is to have one CPU primarily running graphics displays while two CPUs are busy with computations for real-time animation of results.

It should be noted that a 128-MB/sec bus is a very fast bus by today's standards. Only buses that use very exotic technology can go much faster, and these are extremely expensive. So the bus limitation of Titan should not be seen as a liability, but rather a fact of life of today's technology.

6.7.3   SYSTEM BALANCE

Let us examine Titan with respect to the rules of thumb discussed in Chapter 3. A Titan with two CPUs has a computation rate of approximately 9.1 MFLOPS on the 100 by 100 LINPACK benchmark. If we consider a floating-point operation an "instruction" for Titan, Case's ratio and Amdahl's rule (the 1 MB/1 MIPS and 1 Mb I/O/1 MIPS rules with the factor of 8 adjustment for modern systems) conjectures that there should be 73M bytes of memory and 9.1M bytes per second (73M bits) of I/O capacity. Titan actually has 8M to 128M bytes of memory. Titan also has 8M bytes per second of I/O capacity using the SCSI ports, with additional capacity from other I/O devices, so Titan seems to be a well-balanced architecture.

Case's ratio and Amdahl's rule were conjectured in the days before high resolution interactive graphics displays. Titan handles the uncertainty in this area by providing graphics software that allows several options in rendering. The user may choose between slow, realistic drawing modes and fast, simplified drawing modes, so in a sense the balance issue is solved by allowing the user to select an appropriate set of tradeoffs.

Nonetheless, to get a rough feel for Titan's balance in the area of graphics, let us make some simplifying assumptions. If we assume that a screen has 10,000 triangles and is to be redrawn five times per second (for motion, not really fast enough to be called true animation), the machine needs to be able to draw 50,000 triangles per second. Since Titan can draw 47,250 shaded triangles per second (using 400-pixel triangles), this seems to provide good balance at the level of simplified solid-object drawing. Wire-frame graphics, of course, proceed much more quickly, and complex three-dimensional rendering (such as ray tracing) can be much slower.

A good example of system balance in Titan is the balance between the system bus and the memory subsystem capacity. Although the 16-way interleaved memory has some slight excess capacity, in practice the extra number of interleaves reduces bank conflicts and is simpler to decode than a non-power of two, so they are reasonably well matched. Since designing a fast bus is much more difficult than replicating a few more interleaves of memory, it is better to have excess memory capacity than waste bus capacity with too few interleaves of memory.

Another item is the balance between the number of CPUs installed and the capacity of the bus and memory. The fact that CPUs may be installed as options highlights the fact that this is an application-dependent portion of balance. The previous analysis shows that in some code even one CPU can saturate the system resources if it cannot make effective reuse of VRF elements. Experience has shown that it is reasonable to expect the VRF elements to be reused enough to allow two CPUs to be installed. And, in the case of some types of code with appropriate CPU task partitioning, it may be reasonable to have three or four CPUs installed while still maintaining good system balance.

Overall, the Titan system is very well balanced. In particular, the paths over which floating-point operands flow are designed to be fast enough to keep data supplied to the pipelined vector units while at the same time achieving a reasonable tradeoff between cost and performance.

The capacity analysis in this chapter is designed to give the "guaranteed not to exceed" performance of the Titan; in other words, it gives the maximum achievable performance for a stated set of conditions. This analysis is valuable because it gives an upper bound on possible performance for comparison with other machines, but more importantly, it gives a target against which to compare actual program performance. In the next chapter we shall see how real programs perform on Titan.

CHAPTER SEVEN

BENCHMARKS AND PERFORMANCE MEASUREMENT

The architectural analysis of the previous chapter has given us insight into the balance of Titan and the maximum possible performance levels. Now we shall turn our attention to benchmarks and how code is written to take the best advantage of the Titan architecture.

7.1 LINPACK AND LAPACK

The LINPACK benchmark (Dongarra, 1989) is perhaps the most widely-used measurement of floating-point computation performance, especially on high-performance vector machines such as Titan. LINPACK itself is a FORTRAN subroutine library for matrix computation. The LINPACK benchmark is an application of some of the LINPACK subroutines to solve a random 100 by 100 system of simultaneous linear equations. LAPACK is a rewriting of LINPACK to attempt to reduce the memory bandwidth demands of LINPACK for use with machines with vector registers.

7.1.1 LINPACK PERFORMANCE

A LINPACK benchmark result is given in terms of a size and a computation rate. The size is the dimension of the matrix containing the coefficients of the simultaneous equations, with a 100 by 100 element array being the standard case. Larger arrays may be used to demonstrate the effects of a limited size cache or to show how well the peak computation rate is approached as array size increases and relative overhead for loops decreases.

The coefficients in the matrix are randomly generated for the LINPACK benchmark. The computation rate is given in terms of MFLOPS (Millions of Floating Point Operations per Second). For LINPACK, the operations included in the MFLOPS rating are predominantly floating-point multiply and floating-point addition. LINPACK can be given in terms of 32-bit or 64-bit operand computation rates, but the 64-bit computation rates are generally the ones of interest: they will be the only computation rates given here. Because a large portion of code run on supercomputers has the same general characteristics as LINPACK, it is widely considered to be a fair and accurate predictor of supercomputer performance on many scientific code applications.

The heart of the computations performed by the LINPACK benchmark is the operation "Double Precision **A** Times **X** Plus **Y**," or "DAXPY." This operation multiplies the vector **X** times a scalar **A,** then performs a vector addition of that result to the vector **Y**. The "Double" refers to the fact that 64-bit floating-point arithmetic is being performed. DAXPY is the key operation for performing Gaussian Elimination, which is one way of solving systems of linear equations.

Because of the importance of DAXPY, much attention is given to its performance on all supercomputers. In Titan, the DAXPY operation is a single instruction called "DVMA," which is a chained multiply and addition instruction. DVMA uses the VDP to multiply the scalar times the **X** vector, routes the product directly to the adder, then adds the product elements to the **Y** vector. For long vectors, the steady-state computation rate is 16 MFLOPS, because both the adder and the multiplier are kept continuously busy.

In order to perform the DAXPY operation, two vector inputs are needed for the VDP (the **X** and **Y** vectors), and one vector output is produced. For very large arrays, the VRF is ineffectual at buffering elements, because each element of the array is read only one time when performing the computation. Thus, performance at DAXPY is limited if the memory bus cannot keep elements flowing into the VPU. The data requirements of DAXPY are two reads and one write per two floating-point operations.

For a single processor Titan, one read can be processed by the R-BUS for every 16 MHz clock cycle. Because the VPU runs at an 8 MHz operation rate, this provides exactly the two read operands required for every cycle of the VPU. Both a multiplication and an addition of different vector elements are accomplished on each clock cycle, giving an effective 16-MHz

floating-point operation rate. The S-BUS can accommodate twice the number of writes as are required but must share its bandwidth with the IPU
and other system resources.

From this analysis, an infinitely long DAXPY operation should approach
a 16-MFLOPS computation rate on Titan, which is the best that can be
done with the hardware available. Such an operation uses exactly all the
available R-BUS bandwidth with a single CPU and half the available S-BUS
bandwidth. The S-BUS instead of the R-BUS is shared with other hardware, since it is the bus with spare bandwidth. Thus, we can see that Titan
was designed to be a well-balanced DAXPY processor.

Of course, the maximum possible computation rate is not achievable.
The major reason is that the LINPACK benchmark uses finite-sized arrays,
so there is a certain amount of vector startup overhead associated with
each DAXPY pass at a row of the array. The larger the $n^{1/2}$ rating of the
machine (the number of vector elements required to achieve half the peak
performance), the more quickly performance will degrade as the array size
is decreased. Titan's $n^{1/2}$ is reasonably small, so this is not a major performance problem. Another reason that peak performance is not attained in
practice is that LINPACK contains operations other than DAXPY. All
these effects serve to idle the VPU from its peak computation rate for part
of the time.

In order to speed up computations, most supercomputers use replicated
CPUs to perform portions of the LINPACK operations in parallel. If the
operations can be staggered to have one processor performing overhead
computations while another processor performs DAXPY operations, then
the system bus can be kept as busy as possible, bringing the computation
rate closer to the theoretical maximum.

The performance figures for Titan running the LINPACK benchmark
are shown in Table 7.1a. As we can see, performance increases to approach
the peak performance supported by the bus of 16 MFLOPS as processors
are added and as the problem size is increased.

The observation has been made that LINPACK performance corresponds closely to available bus bandwidth. This is because the vector operations in LINPACK demand all their operands from memory, and most
supercomputers have an architecture which permits adding processors to
the point that memory bandwidth is largely consumed when running LIN-
PACK for best results. For example, on Titan, the 16 MFLOPS attainable
DAXPY rate is limited by R-BUS performance, so this is the maximum
attainable rate no matter how many processors are added.

Some designs have taken to adding very large cache memories to
improve LINPACK performance. If the entire array fits into the cache,

TABLE 7.1.　Titan LINPACK and LAPACK performance

(a) LINPACK MFLOPS	NUMBER OF PROCESSORS			
size	1	2	3	4
100 × 100	6.5	9.1	11.0	11.7
300 × 300	9.0	13.4	14.7	15.0
1000 × 1000	10.5	15.0	15.6	15.7
(b) LAPACK MFLOPS	NUMBER OF PROCESSORS			
size	1	2	3	4
100 × 100	6.1	9.1	10.6	11.2
300 × 300	10.4	18.4	24.6	28.6
1000 × 1000	13.1	25.5	36.5	46.6

then performance may be quite good; however, as soon as the size of the array of coefficients exceeds the amount of cache memory, performance degrades markedly (Stone, 1987).

7.1.2　LAPACK PERFORMANCE

The memory demands of LINPACK can be solved in one of two ways. The first way is architectural support in the form of more raw bus bandwidth. Unfortunately, this method tends to be too expensive to be practical beyond a certain cost/performance tradeoff point for any design. The second method available is to change the algorithm to make it consume less bus bandwidth.

LAPACK is a set of numerical subroutines which is designed to perform identically to LINPACK while providing better performance on vector floating-point processors. LAPACK accomplishes its goal by loading small blocks of the coefficient matrix into vector registers, then performing as many operations as possible on these quantities before generating more memory traffic. To the extent that LAPACK is functionally identical to LINPACK, it offers a "free" speedup mechanism for existing architectures.

The "trick" of changing the algorithm to provide better speedup is available in many situations. In general, an algorithm improvement (if one can be found) is always more desirable than more complicated hardware, because the costs to distribute an existing algorithm are quite low, whereas the per-unit production costs of hardware are reasonably high.

Because LAPACK reduces demands on bus bandwidth, it allows more vector processing units to be connected to a given bus before the bus becomes saturated. Another way of looking at this is that adding more VPUs to Titan bus does not generate as much interfering bus traffic when using LAPACK, so better performance improvements may be expected than when using LINPACK. Table 7.1b shows performance for LAPACK on Titan.

7.2   ELEMENTARY FUNCTIONS

We have just discussed a performance area where vector machines are at their best—the DAXPY operation, but there are other sections of code that are crucial to system performance over a variety of applications that are not so easily vectorized. One of the most difficult (and important) of these areas is the computation of elementary functions.

The elementary functions (sine, cosine, natural logarithm, etc.) are requirements for graphics transformations and other important calculations. The problem is that standard means of computing these functions in a naive manner (e.g., using Taylor expansion series) requires division and numerous conditional branches, both of which prohibit efficient vectorization of code. In order to solve these problems, Titan uses a specially developed math function library. The math library does not attempt to use the vector hardware to speed up individual function computations, but rather attempts to speed up the computation of vectors of function calculations.

Division is a much slower operation than multiplication on most high-performance processors. In Titan, the hardware division unit of the VDP is not pipelinable and so runs a factor of eight times slower than the multiplier unit in terms of throughput. The elimination of division from elementary function calculations is a well-known practice, and the descriptions of how this is done are widely available (Cody and Waite, 1980).

The other problem, the one of conditional branches, stems from the fact that most schemes for computing elementary functions are based on approximations for limited values of inputs. For example, sine and cosine approximations may only be available for input values of 0 to 45 degrees ($\pi/4$ radians). The problem is then to reduce the range of the given argument to one which fits the available approximations.

We shall now follow the operations required to compute cosine as an example of how such operations are done. In each step, it is a vector operation which is being performed. We assume a vector ϕ of input angles and an output vector of cosine values as a result. The approach used is simplistic for the sake of clarity and shows the different ways that a vector machine can be made to execute difficult code. It does not necessarily represent the efficient proprietary approach used in the actual Titan math library.

The input to cosine, in radians, can be any positive or negative value. In order to apply available approximations, we must reduce the input to a range of 0 to $\pi/2$ radians. First, we shall reduce the input range from all numbers to non-negative numbers using the trigonometric identity

$$\cos(\phi) = \cos(-\phi).$$

This can be done with a simple absolute-value vector instruction. This instruction buries the conditional based on sign within the operation of the instruction itself.

Next, the value of ϕ could be reduced to a range of 0 to 2π radians using the identity

$$\cos(\phi) = \cos(\phi + 2\pi * k),$$

where k is an integer. An obvious technique to do this is to get the remainder when ϕ is divided by 2π. A way to accomplish this is to multiply ϕ by $1/(2\pi)$ (equivalent to dividing by 2π), take the fractional portion, then multiply the result by 2π. Since this remaindering process works even for values less than 2π, no conditionals are needed. Titan has various "int" instructions which can be used to subtract the integer portion from a number, leaving the remainder.

Once the argument range is reduced to the interval $(0, 2\pi)$, we subtract ϕ from 2π if ϕ is greater than π. This takes advantage of the symmetry of the cosine function about the input value π:

$$\cos(\phi) = \cos(2\pi - \phi); \qquad \pi \le \phi \le 2\pi.$$

In order to perform this reduction, we must first compare all elements of the vector with π, then perform a subtraction only on those elements greater than π. This is performed with a vector compare instruction followed by a subtract under mask instruction. The subtract under mask will only affect those elements for which the mask bit is set, where the mask bit is only set for those elements greater than π.

Similarly, we can use the symmetry of cosine about the value $\pi/2$ to further reduce the range to the interval to $[0, \pi/2]$. The identity involved is

$$\cos(\phi) = -\cos(\pi - \phi); \qquad \pi/2 \le \phi \le \pi.$$

It is important to note that there is a sign change here. In scalar code, this sign change would involve either a conditional branch or, more likely, saving a variable someplace with a sign to be applied to the output. In a vector machine, we have the additional choice of saving the vector mask that was applied to perform the subtraction and later using this same vector mask to perform a negation under mask.

There is one range reduction left. Some efficient series for cosine are only accurate from 0 to $\pi/4$ radians, and our cosine argument cannot easily be reduced to less than $\pi/2$ radians. Fortunately, there is an efficient implementation for sine that is also accurate from 0 to $\pi/4$ radians, and we have the trigonometric identity:

$$\sin(\phi) = \cos(\pi/4 - \phi).$$

After another masked subtraction, we have fully-reduced arguments that must be input as arguments to either a sine or cosine approximation series. (Let us say a simple Chebyshev series is used.) One way of performing this operation using vectors is to compute the series twice under mask, once for sine, and once for cosine. Another potentially more efficient mechanism is to build customized vectors of coefficients where each vector of coefficients has elements pulled from a list for either sine or cosine, depending on whether the argument needs the sine or cosine calculation. In this way, all the computations could proceed at once.

After the series computation is completed, the answer is available upon adjusting the sign as mentioned earlier. One area we have not touched on, but which is of vital importance, is controlling round-off error to return accurate results.

7.3 THE P3 MODIFICATIONS FOR IMPROVED PERFORMANCE

The overall performance goal of the Titan project was a significant fraction of the performance of a Cray-class supercomputer at high-end workstation prices. Table 7.2 shows r^∞ and $n^{1/2}$ values (which are defined in Chapter 3)

TABLE 7.2.   Titan versus Cray X-MP vector characteristics.

Operation	Titan		Cray	
	r^∞	$n^{1/2}$	r^∞	$n^{1/2}$
$v = v + s$	7.48 MFLOPS	7.7	76.6 MFLOPS	15
$v = v * v$	6.32 MFLOPS	7.3	68.7 MFLOPS	25
$v = s + v * v$	11.68 MFLOPS	6.7	102 MFLOPS	13
$v = s * v + v$	14.5 MFLOPS	18.0		

for Titan and a Cray X-MP for the given operations, taking into account the mix of memory and vector register accesses encountered in a simple FORTRAN loop. In these examples, v is a vector quantity, and s is a scalar quantity. Table 7.3 shows that for basic operations, Titan is about one-tenth the speed of a Cray X-MP, with slightly better relative performance on short-vector code (which tends to dominate many computations). The primary reason that the Titan is significantly slower than the Cray is that it uses much less exotic (and therefore much less expensive) technology, resulting in a significantly longer clock-cycle time. As discussed in Chapter 1, even 10% of the performance of a large supercomputer is adequate for Titan, since it is a small single-user supercomputer instead of a large, shared mainframe.

Of course, there are areas in which Titan could be better. The first major upgrade to Titan is in the form of the "P3" processor (sold as the Stardent 3000), which incorporates new technology and some design enhancements to improve performance that was introduced approximately one year after the introduction of the first processor version.

The easiest way to make a system faster is by increasing the clock speed. Because the R2000 chip was chosen as the IPU, the P3 processor uses an R3000 component which runs at 33 MHz instead of the original 16 MHz IPU. The VDP floating-point chips have been replaced with 33 MHz components (with 16.5 MHz pipeline stage times) as well, which maintains the two-to-one ratio of IPU cycle time to VPU cycle time. In addition the MIPS R3010 scalar floating-point coprocessor has been added. This allows the R3000 to perform scalar floating-point operations without using the VPU, greatly reducing latency.

Another obvious area for performance improvement is in the capacity of the system bus. The system bus was built as wide and as fast as possible with the technology available at the time. Unfortunately, technology must progress significantly for the bus itself to be made faster because of elec-

TABLE 7.3.   Titan vs Cray X-MP vector performance.

Operation	MFLOPS Titan	MFLOPS Cray X-MP
short (length = 10)		
$v = v + s$	2.31	14.4
$v = v * v$	2.17	14.0
$v = v * v + v * v$	3.84	33.5
long (length = 500 for Titan, 1000 for Cray)		
$v = v + s$	7.98	76.6
$v = v * v$	6.48	68.7
$v = v * v + v * v$	9.58	115.2

trical loading and propagation time considerations, however, several aspects of the bus can be made to speed up real performance (as opposed to theoretical maximum performance). The most important of these aspects is a reduction in the latency in IPU and VPU control logic for loading an element from memory in P3.

A third area for performance improvement is with compiler technology. The P3 version of the FORTRAN compiler is augmented to include loop unrolling for scalar code, more comprehensive code rearrangement for better load/store latency management, and optimizations involving use of the accumulators in the VDP.

Other features that have been added to the P3 version for better performance include

· A pipelined hardware division unit for better throughput on code that makes use of vector divide instructions;
· Hardware support for square roots (part of the hardware divide unit);
· Larger caches for the IPU (64K bytes each for the instruction and data caches);
· A larger ETLB with 32K entries for better hit ratios for the VPU;
· More bandwidth for the VRF to eliminate stalls for write conflicts. This eliminates much of the control logic for handling pipeline stalling in the VDP;
· Use of faster chips for the VDP, reducing latency to two cycles;
· Simplification of the operation pipe. Halting and restart of the pipeline was a complex operation in P2. No customers were found that required this functionality and hence it was eliminated;
· Hardware support for integer vector instructions, which were specified but not implemented on earlier hardware versions;
· Use of larger and faster gate array chips (reduced gate delay from 3 *nsec* to 1.5 *nsec*) to reduce interchip propagation delays. For example, the two VPU gate arrays are combined into a single, larger gate area for P3, and
· Reduced latency for some operations, including cache miss processing, vector instruction issue, and vector operation scoreboarding.

A final feature which will be added to P3 is hardware support for scatter/gather. Scatter/gather is the capability of loading or storing a vector made up of irregularly dispersed elements of a data structure for techniques such as sparse matrix manipulation. A typical means for doing this operation in FORTRAN would be code using indirect indices of the form

$$A(X(J)) = B(Y(J)) + C(Z(J)).$$

Scatter/gather support for P2 was done using code in the IPU. For P3, this feature will be supported by special hardware in the VPU load-and-store pipes for greater speed.

Design and testing methodology were also modified for P3. Logic synthesis replaced hand-generated logic design. A logic synthesizer compatible with the Verilog description language was selected. Not only was textual description more simple than schematic capture, there was no need to validate that the gate-level design and the register-transfer level description were consistent.

In review, the testing strategy for P2 consisted of four parts:

Functional test to verify the Principles of Operation. These tests were written by hand.

Tests to exercise internal functions. Example internal operations include scoreboard hazard detection, arbitration for the vector register file, etc. These tasks typically exercise a single function but require several concurrent operations for setup. The tests were written by hand but generated by program.

Tests that exercise interactions between modules. These tests exercise the interfaces between modules. The tests were generated at random using a test generator. A set of operations was selected at random, and their results were predicted by the test generator.

Simulation of actual code. In P3, the test strategy was modified to rely more heavily on test generators for internal functional tests. The random test generation was expanded to include the integer and vector units. The major change, however, was the elimination of simulation of actual code. Rather, pieces of the logic were exhaustively simulated in isolation. The

TABLE 7.4.   Comparison of the VPU design process.

	P2	P3
Number of ASICs	9	4
Total gates designed	103K	110K
Number synthesized	5K	88K
Number hand-designed	98K	22K
Number of tests		
Basic operations	16	24
Internal functions	13	109
Random	178	376
Total	207	509
Number of test simulation cycles (millions)	2.25	7.81
Elapsed design time (months)	17	10
Total design effort (man-months)	106	57

possible number of test states was reduced by using the knowledge of the environment in which the logic was embedded. Monitors were also inserted into the simulation model. Anytime an insertion about the model encoded in the monitors was violated, a flag was raised and the simulation was halted. Table 7.4 compares attributes of the P2 and P3 design processes. Less than 5% of the vector-processing unit gates were synthesized automatically in P2 compared with over 80% in P3. Almost two and one-half times more tests were simulated and the time to market, as well as the man-months of effort, was almost cut in half.

7.4 THE ELEVEN RULES OF SUPERCOMPUTER DESIGN

In a videotaped lecture (Bell, 1989), C. Gordon Bell listed 11 rules of supercomputer design. They sum up the lessons learned from the Titan experience. These are annotated here in light of the discussions of previous chapters.

(1) **Performance, performance, performance.** People are buying supercomputers for performance. Performance, within a broad range, is everything. Thus, performance goals for Titan were increased during the initial design phase even though it increased the target selling price; furthermore, the focus on the second-generation Titan was on increasing performance above all else.

(2) **Everything matters.** The use of the harmonic mean for reporting performance on the Livermore Loops severely penalizes machines that run poorly on even one loop. It also brings little benefit for those loops that run significantly faster than other loops. Since the Livermore Loops was designed to simulate the real computational load mix at Livermore Labs, there can be no holes in performance when striving to achieve high performance on this realistic mix of computational loads.

(3) **Scalars matter the most.** A well-designed vector unit will probably be fast enough to make scalars the limiting factor. Even if scalar operations can be issued efficiently, high latency through a pipelined floating-point unit such as the VPU can be deadly in some applications. The P3 Titan improved scalar performance by using the MIPS R3010 scalar floating-point coprocessing chip. This significantly reduced overhead and latency for scalar operations.

(4) **Provide as much vector performance as price allows.** Peak vector performance is primarily determined by bus bandwidth in some circumstances and the use of vector registers in others. Thus the bus was designed to be as fast as practical using a cost-effective mix of TTL and ECL logic, and the VRF was designed to be as large and flexible as possible within cost limitations. Gordon Bell's rule of thumb is that each vector unit must be able to produce at least two results per clock tick to have acceptably high performance.

(5) **Avoid holes in the performance space.** This is an amplification of rule 2. Certain specific operations may not occur often in an "average" application, but in those applications where they occur, lack of high-speed support can significantly degrade performance. An example of this in P2 is the slow divide unit. A pipelined divide unit was added to the P3 version of Titan because one particular benchmark code (Flo82) made extensive use of division.

(6) **Place peaks in performance.** Marketing sells machines as much as or more so than technical excellence. Benchmark and specification wars are inevitable; therefore, the most important inner loops or benchmarks for the targeted market should be identified, and inexpensive methods should be used to increase performance. It is vital that the system can be called the "World's Fastest," even though only on a single program. A typical way that this is done is to build special optimizations into the compiler to recognize specific benchmark programs. Titan is able to do well on programs that can make repeated use of a long vector stored in one of its vector register files.

(7) **Provide a decade of addressing.** Computers never have enough address space. History is full of examples of computers that have run out of memory-addressing space for important applications while still relatively early in their life (e.g., the PDP-8, the IBM System 360, and the IBM PC). Ideally, a system should be designed to last for 10 years without running out of memory-address space for the maximum amount of memory that can be installed. Since dynamic RAM chips tend to quadruple in size every three years, this means that the address space should contain seven bits more than required to address installed memory on the initial system. A first-generation Titan with fully loaded memory cards uses 27 bits of address space, while only 29 bits of address lines are available on the system bus. When 16M bit DRAM chips become available, Titan will be limited by its bus design and not by real estate on its memory boards.

(8) **Make it easy to use.** The "dusty deck" syndrome, in which users want to reuse FORTRAN code written two or three decades earlier, is ram-

pant in the supercomputer world. Supercomputers with parallel processors and vector units are expected to run this code efficiently without any work on the part of the programmer. While this may not be entirely realistic, it points out the issue of making a complex system easy to use. Technology changes too quickly for customers to have time to become an expert on each and every machine version.

(9) **Build on others' work.** One mistake on the first version of Titan was to "reinvent the wheel" in the case of the IPU compiler. Stardent should have relied more heavily on the existing MIPS compiler technology and used its resources in areas where it could add value to existing MIPS work (such as in the area of multiprocessing).

(10) **Design for the next one and then do it again.** In a small start-up company, resources are always scarce, and survival depends on shipping the next product on schedule. It is often difficult to look beyond the current design, yet this is vital for long-term success. Extra care must be taken in the design process to plan ahead for future upgrades. The best way to do this is to start designing the next generation before the current generation is complete, using a pipelined hardware design process. Also, be resigned to throwing away the first design as quickly as possible.

(11) **Have slack resources.** Expect the unexpected. No matter how good the schedule, unscheduled events will occur. It is vital to have spare resources available to deal with them, even in a startup company with little extra manpower or capital.

A final comment from (Bell, 1989) is that supercomputers are extremely complex and difficult to build. It takes $50 million to design and ship a product for a small-scale supercomputer start-up company. The entry cost is high, and the job is tough, but the team at Stardent has shown that it can be done successfully.

THE TITAN BUS

A.1 INTRODUCTION

The Titan R-Bus and S-Bus formed the backbone of the system. Each bus operates at 16 MHz with the capability of transfering eight bytes with each clock tick, yielding a maximum potential throughput of 128 Mbytes per second. The R (or Read) BUS is used exclusively for vector read traffic. The S-BUS is used for the integer processor, graphics processor, and input/output, read/write memory transactions. Since only the S-BUS may be used for writes, each processor can maintain cache coherency by monitoring this single bus. To increase throughput, a synchronous split-transaction bus protocol is used. For writes, there is a fixed delay between the appearance of the address and the data on the bus. For reads, however, the response time is variable. Thus the read operation is composed of two separate bus cycles: the first portion places the address onto the bus, and sometime later the second portion returns the data. Between the first and second portions of the bus transaction, the bus may be used by other devices.

Since the operation of the R-BUS is a proper subset of the S-BUS, we will consider its operation in the following discussion. The S-BUS supports four transaction types:

· Sub-word, single word, or double word memory read,
· Sub-word, single word, or double word memory write,

181

- Memory load and sync, and
- Memory scrub.

The bus transactions can be initiated by the integer processor, floating-point unit, graphics processor, or I/O processor. The R and S buses are each composed of three sub-buses: data bus, address bus, and control bus. The two buses share an arbitration bus and a clock bus. There are a total of 358 signals in these eight buses. Table A-1 summarizes the signals in the data and address buses. The data bus is composed of a four-byte data low and a four-byte data high subfield, each protected by byte parity. To take advantage of dynamic memory "static-column" capability, four bytes are placed on the data low sub-bus during the first clock period while the four high-order bytes are placed on the data high lines during the next clock period. The address bus supplies a 32-bit byte address used in the transaction. A cycle request signal indicates the start of a new transaction. The read line indicates whether the operation is a read or a write. The requester number indicates the originator of the bus operation (i.e., one of four processors), the graphics processor, or an I/O request. The cycle-type and access-type fields specify the transaction type and size. Finally, a parity bit protects the information supplied on the address bus.

The control bus provides hand-shaking, interrupt, and error-control signals and is summarized in Table A-2. Whereas the cycle request signal on the address bus indicates the requesters start of bus transaction, the cycle-acknowledge on the control bus is provided by the responder and indicated that it will respond. Data valid signals indicate that information on

TABLE A.1.   Summary of R/S data and address bus.

Data Bus	
Data lo $<31:0>$	- low order four bytes of data
Data hi $<31:0>$	- high order four bytes of data
Byte parity low$<3:0>$	- parity for low order four bytes of data
Byte parity hi $<3:0>$	- parity for high order four bytes of data
Address Bus	
Cycle request	- indicates start of new transaction
Address$<31:0>$	- byte address for transaction
Read	- indicates whether transaction is read or write
Requester number$<7:0>$	- identity of requester that initiated transaction
Cycle type$<1:0>$	- indicates type of transaction (eg., single/subword, double word, indivisible)
Access type$<1:0>$	- indicates size of transaction (eg., one, two, three, or four bytes)
Parity	- parity over all fields of the Address Bus

TABLE A.2.   Summary of R/S control bus.

Control Bus	
Cycle acknowledge	-responder indicates it recognized request and will respond
Data valid low	-memory read data on Data Lo Bus is valid
Data valid hi	-memory read data on Data Hi Bus is valid
Return ID	-identity of requester currently supplying Data Lo Bus
Return ID parity	-parity over Return ID field
Slot ID<3:0>	-a constant that provides the number of the slot in which the board is inserted
Interleave	-indicates whether memory is 8 or 16 way interleaved
Interrupt<3:0>	-four levels of interrupt sent to all processors
Error interrupt<3:0>	-force interrupt on one of four processors
Boot error	-interrupt processor designated to boot system
Powerfail	-asserted 15 milliseconds before power loss
Reset<1:0>	-clear certain status registers due to either power-on reset or processor initiated reset

the data bus is valid. The return-ID field identifies the current driver of the data bus. The slot-ID field is a constant used by the processors to uniquely identify themselves. The interleave signal informs the various cards in the system as to whether the memory is configured as an 8- or 16-way interleave. The interrupts are bused to all processors on four different hardware priority levels. An error interrupt is directed to one of the four processors when errors are encountered during an operation it requested. More serious error conditions inform the boot processor to reinitialize the system through the boot error signal. Power fail and reset lines complete the control-bus specification.

The arbitration and clock buses are shared by the R and S buses. All the bus signals described so far are implemented in TTL logic. Since the bus cycle time is determined by the propagation delay of both the arbitration and clock signals, these buses are implemented with ECL (Emittor-Coupled Logic). Table A-3 summarizes the signals on these buses. Each potential bus master has a request line. Each of the potential responders has a corresponding busy signal. In order to make full utilization of the bus, requesters are not granted permission to use the bus unless the resources they request are available to respond. The arbitration sync line ensures that the round-robin priority scheme works correctly. The clock bus distributes the system clock at twice the frequency of bus operation. A clock-sync B signal ensures that the bus clocks derived from the system clock maintain the same phase. Finally, an enable signal is used to gate other signals onto the bus. The next section illustrates how these bus signals are used to implement the various transaction types.

TABLE A.3.   Summary of arbitration and clock buses.

Arbitration Bus	
Bus request<8:1>	-one line for each bus requester
Busy	-signals which indicate a resource is busy:
	interleave<15:0>
	I/O
	graphics
	read
Arbitration sync	-ensures that rotating priority counters in each requester stay in sync
Clock Bus	
System clock	-32 MHz clock for all cards
Clock-sync B	-used to ensure the 16 MHz bus clocks derived from the 32 MHz system clock stay in phase
Enable	-signal to enable other signals onto the bus

A.2 WRITE AND READ BUS TRANSACTIONS

Figure A-1 (a) illustrates the activities on the arbitration, address, data, and control buses for each clock period for a double word-write operation. The transaction starts when a requester realizes it will require a system resource. The initiator of the request signals its intention to its local arbitration circuit. The arbitration circuit determines whether the resource requested will be available after two clock periods (i.e., the quickest that a request will arrive at a resouce is two clock periods—one for arbitration and one for the bus transfer). If the resource will be free, the arbiter will grant access to the initiator to the local bus. At the same time, the arbiter places the bus request on the system bus. Each local arbiter samples the global bus request and selects itself if it has the highest priority during this arbitration cycle. The winner of the arbitration cycle will get the global bus during the next clock period. The local arbiter issues the busy signal for the appropriate resource for the present and the next two clock periods until the responder is capable of asserting it on its own. For the write transaction, the arbiter must be sure that both the address and data bus will be free. On cycle i in Figure A-1 (a) the bus has been granted and the interleave busy signal for the selected memory resource is asserted. During clock period $i + 1$ the address, the requester number, type of transaction, and the low data word are placed on the address and data buses. The cycle request line indicates that the address and data buses are valid. On cycle

		i	i + 1	i + 2	i + 3
Arbitration	Arbitrate	Interleave Busy	Interleave Busy	Interleave Busy	Interleave Busy
Address			Cycle Req Address Type Req Num		
Data			Data Lo	Data Hi	
Control					Cycle Ack

(a) Write

		i	i + 1	i + 2	i + 3						
Arbitration	Arbitrate	Interleave Busy	Interleave Busy	Interleave Busy			Arbitrate	Read Busy	Read Busy	Read Busy	Read Busy
Address			Cycle Req Address Type Req Num			• • •					
Data										Data Lo	Data Hi
Control					Cycle Ack Return ID					Data Valid Lo Return ID	Data Valid Hi Return ID

(b) Read

FIGURE A.1. System-bus write/read operations.

$i + 2$ the second data word (if any) is placed on a data bus. During cycle $i + 3$ the arbiter is no longer responsible for asserting interleave busy. The responder must assert interleave busy and cycle-acknowledge on the control bus. If there is no cycle-acknowledge then a non-existent address error is indicated to either the initiating or boot processor.

The read bus transaction is depicted in Figure A1(b). The arbitration and next four clock cycles are essentially identical to the write operation except that the initiator does not place any information on the data bus. At some time later the responder arbitrates for the bus and asserts read-busy two cycles before it places read data on the data bus. This effectively reserves the bus for the returning read data. The requester monitors the return ID and data-valid low bus signals. If the data-valid low and the appropriate return ID are not seen within 1024 clocks, the initiator logs a time-out exception to the initiating or boot processor and terminates the transaction. If the data-valid low and appropriate return ID are received within the specified time, the data on the data-low bus is considered to be good. Another clock cycle is used to return data high if a double word transaction was initially requested.

A.3 OTHER TRANSACTION TYPES

The load-and-sync bus operation is used to implement semaphores. The load-and-sync is essentially identical to the read transaction except the word that has been read from memory is modified. If the word read from memory is positive, it is replaced by zero; otherwise, the word read from memory is incremented and written back.

The memory-scrub transaction is an indivisible read-correct-write sequence that is used to correct a potential single-bit error in a word before a second soft error may occur in that word. Any write data transferred on the bus is ignored.

A.4 ERROR DETECTION AND HANDLING

Each data bus carries even byte parity. For parity checking purposes, the return ID is considered part of the data bus for reads and is covered by the return parity bit. Parity is considered valid for read data whenever the appropriate data-valid signal is asserted. In addition, parity is considered valid when there is a valid write request on the bus. Each request and address field also carries even byte parity. These parity bits are considered valid whenever the corresponding cycle request signal is asserted.

The goal is to detect and signal exceptions as soon as possible after their occurrence. Whenever possible, the software process that initiated an operation that resulted in an exception should be signaled and is responsible for initiating recovery. If this is not possible, the processor that initiated an operation that resulted in an exception is signaled and is responsible for initiating recovery. Certain I/O and graphics processor exceptions may be detected with no information as to which processor initiated the transaction. In this case, the boot processor is interrupted.

The exception-handling mechanism is uniform and independent of source. When an exception condition is detected, it is logged in the status register. A level-five interrupt is signaled to the appropriate processor. The processor is executing a synchronous operation and is therefore stalled; a processor bus error is also asserted. When the exception is serviced, the bit signaling the exception is cleared.

On a read exception, the bus specification states that bad parity is returned on all data bytes. This is due to the fact that the integer processors read synchronously and are stalled. The IPU is not listening for interrupts, and the processor is stopped on the offending instruction. Returning bad parity on the data forces a data-parity error at the initiator and allows the normal bus read protocol to be followed. Thus the processor must check the responder after a failed transaction due to a parity error to determine whether the error was caused by a broken bus or by the responder.

There are two classes of errors that make a correct response impossible: a parity error on the request number field and parity error on the transaction-type field. In the first case, the responder cannot be certain who made the request. In the second case, the responder cannot be sure if the request was a read or a write. In both cases, the responder logs the error and provides no further response. The result will be a non-existent address (NXA) error. The cause of the NXA signal (i.e., due to non-existent memory reference or a request number for a transaction-type parity error) is determined by reading all system-bus status registers.

If an initiator sees a transaction with a parity error on the return ID field, the initiator sets the request-parity error bit in the bus status register. No further action is taken, and as a result the transaction is lost. At some future time the initiator will time out. Thus the initiator of the broken transaction will be responsible for carrying through the error protocol. Note that the bus time-out indicator is now ambiguous in that it may be caused when there is no response or because of a parity error on the return ID field. The cause of the bus time-out is determined by reading the bus status registers.

The bus protocol allows for a retransmission of read data by responders if a correctable error occurs. If an error is detected, the data-valid low signal is stalled until the responder can correct the bad data. Then the normal return portion of the read-bus transaction is followed. If a correctable error is detected on the data-high information, both the low and high data are retransmitted.

TITAN P2 SPECIFICATION SUMMARY

System Statistics

Number of processors	1–4
Physical address space	512 Mbyte
Virtual address space	2G byte
Bus width	6 bytes
Bus bandwidth	256 Mbytes/sec
Memory size	8 M–128 Mbytes
Memory access time (64 bits)	8 cycles
Memory recovery time (64 bits)	2 cycles
Memory cycle time (64 bits)	10 cycles
Memory interleaving	8- or 16-way
I/O disk channels	2 @ 4 Mbyte/sec
I/O VME bandwidth	15 Mbyte/sec
Screen resolution	1280 × 1024
Pixel resolution	24 bit full-color
Screen refresh rate	60 Hz
Gouraud shading rate	200K 3D triangles/sec
Vector drawing rate	400K 3D vectors/sec
Memory/screen block transfer	5.2 Mpixels/sec
Screen/screen block transfer	7 Mpixels/sec
380 MB internal disks	1–3

LINPACK performance   6.1 MFLOPS
   (100 × 100 64-bit compiled 1 processor)
LINPACK performance   15.7 MFLOPS
   (1000 × 1000 64-bit compiled 4 processors)
LAPACK performance   46.6 MFLOPS
   (1000 × 1000 64-bit compiled 4 processors)

Processor Statistics

MIPS per processor (peak)	16
MIPS per processor (avg.)	10
Vector unit pipe rate	8 MHz
Floating-point rate (peak)	16 MFLOPS
Floating-point rate (avg.)	6 MFLOPS
Number of memory pipes	2 load, 1 store
Number of operation units	3
Load latency	8 cycles
Store latency	2 cycles
Operation latency	6 cycles
$n^{1/2}$ $(v = s * v + v)$	18 elements
r^{∞} $(v = s * v + v)$	14.5 MFLOPS
Livermore loops	1.7 MFLOPS
(length 16, harmonic mean)	
Integer registers	32
Vector register sets	8 (variable)
Vector register length	32 (variable)

Other Characteristics

IEEE 32- and 64-bit floating-point format
Parity-checked synchronous bus and cache
SECMED error-correcting memory
16-bit Z-buffer
Diagnostic port on each processor

APPENDIX C

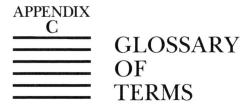

GLOSSARY
OF
TERMS

ALU	- Arithmetic and Logic Unit
AOP	- A OPerand for VDP
access time	- time required to read or write a value to or from memory
BOP	- B OPerand for VDP
bandwidth	- information flow capacity per unit time
block size	- the number of bytes
COP	- C OPerand for VDP
CPU	- Central Processing Unit
cache coherency	- the property of caches that copies of a data element in different caches must all have the same value
cache capacity	- the number of bytes of memory in the cache memory
chaining	- using results of one vector operation directly for another operation without intermediate storage (and allowing the second operation to proceed as soon as each element of the first operation is available)
DMA	- Direct Memory Access
DRSLT	- "Division Result" bus of VDP
display list	- a sequence of commands stored in program memory to be executed by the GPU

dual ported   - memory with two access ports allowing two simul-
                         taneous memory operations
ETLB   - External Translation Lookaside Buffer
FIFO   - First-In/First-Out buffer
GB   - GigaBytes
GPU   - Graphics Processing Unit
Gouraud   - a type of 3D graphics shading
harmonic mean   - average which is the reciprocal of the sum of the
                         reciprocals
hazard detection   - detection of data dependency situations which
                         could cause incorrect vector operation (e.g.,
                         ensuring a write is not performed to a location
                         until all data reads from that location have
                         completed)
IPU   - Integer Processing Unit
interleave   - a partition of physical memory used to increase
                         available bandwidth
locality   - the tendency of programs to access the same loca-
                         tion repeatedly (temporal locality), or to access
                         adjacent locations in sequence (spatial locality)
MB/sec   - MegaByte per second
MBP   - Multiplier ByPass input to the VDP
MFLOPS   - Million Floating-Point Operations Per Second
MRSLT   - "Multiplier Result" bus of VDP
MWords   - Million 64-bit Words
memory cycle time   - the complete time to access a memory element,
                         including access and recovery time
ns   - nanosecond(s)
$n^{1/2}$ - the length of a vector that achieves one-half the
                         r^{∞} computation rate
pipeline   - a method by which computations are broken
                         down into steps, allowing different steps of dif-
                         ferent computations to proceed simultaneously
pseudocolor   - colors on the screen are selected from a limited
                         palette of colors
R-BUS   - Read Bus
rasterizer   - special-purpose hardware to speed up drawing
rendering   - the process of producing a drawing from a collec-
                         tion of data, often as a three-dimensional
                         projection
r^{∞} - the maximum possible instruction execution rate
                         for an infinite length vector
S-BUS   - Store Bus

SCSI   - Small Computer System Interface standard
SECMED   - Single Error Correction, Multiple Error detection
SPICE   - "Simulation Program, Integrated Circuits Emphasis"
STRIFE   - "Stress/Life," a form of system testing that involves operating at conditions exceeding the recommended limits in order to find weak components.
scalar operations   - operations on single data elements
scoreboard   - a hardware control mechanism for maintaining the status of ongoing operations, used for chaining and hazard detection
set size   - the number of sets in a cache memory
spin-lock   - a semaphore for synchronization which is accessed by repeated reading until its value changes to "unlocked"
stalling   - stopping the execution of a processor until some error or resource contention situation is resolved
TLB   - Translation Lookaside Buffer (a cache of the most recently accessed mappings of virtual address space to physical address space)
UART   - Universal Asynchronous Receiver/Transmitter (also known as a "serial port" or ACIA)
VCU   - Vector Control Unit
VDP   - Vector Data Path
VDS   - Vector Data Switch
VME   - The "Versa Module Europa" system bus standard
VPU   - Vector Processor Unit
VRF   - Vector Register File
vector   - a data structure consisting of a one-dimensional array of elements having identical data types
vector operations   - operations that take place on the elements of a vector (as opposed to scalar operations, which are performed on a single data element)
working set   - the data and instructions accessed by a program in a relatively short period of time, typically corresponding to data resident in a cache memory (or, for longer periods of time, that part of the virtual address space resident in physical memory)
Z-buffer   - a graphics buffer that holds the "depth" value of each pixel for hidden surface elimination

REFERENCES

Allen, R. (1988). Unifying Vectorization, Parallelization, and Optimization: The Ardent Compiler, Third International Conference on Supercomputing and Second World Supercomputer Exhibition, May 15–20.

Allen, R., and Johnson, S. (1988). Compiling C for Vectorization, Parallelization, and Inline Expansion, Proceedings of the SIGPLAN Conference on Programming Language Design and Implementation.

Amdahl, G. M. (1967). Validity of the Single Processor Approach to Achieving Large-Scale Computing Capabilities, in: 1967 Spring Joint Computing Conf., *AFIPS Conf. Proc.* Vol. 30 (Thompson, ed.). Washington, DC, 483.

Bell, C. G. (1989). The 11 Rules of Supercomputer Design, Distinguished Lecture Series, Vol. II, videotape, University Video Communications, Stanford, CA.

Bell, C. G., Miranker, G. S., and Rubinstein, J. J. (1988). Solo Supercomputing, *IEEE Spectrum* **25**(4), 46–50.

Borden, B. S. (1989). Graphics Processing on a Graphics Supercomputer, *IEEE Computer Graphics and Applications* **9**(4), 56–62.

Bresenham, J. E. (1965). Algorithm for Computer Control of a Digital Plotter, *IBM Systems J.* **4(1),** 25–30.

Cody, W. J., and Waite, W. (1980). "Software Manual for the Elementary Functions." Prentice Hall, Englewood Cliffs, NJ.

Curnow, H. J., and Wichmann, B. A. (1976). A Synthetic Benchmark, *The Computer J.* **19(1).**

Denning, P. J. (1970). Virtual Memory, *Computing Surveys,* **2**(3), 153–189.

Diede, T., Hagenmaier, C. F., Miranker, G. S., Rubinstein, J. J., and Worley, W. S. Jr. (1988). The Tital Graphics Supercomputer Architecture, *IEEE Computer* **21**(9), 13–30.

195

Dongarra, J. (1989). Performance of Various Computers Using Standard Linear Equations Software in a Fortran Environment, Technical Memorandum No. 23, Argonne National Laboratory, June 4.

Dongarra, J., Martin, J. L., and Worlton, J. (1987). Computer benchmarking: Paths and Pitfalls. *IEEE Spectrum*, **24**, 38–43.

Farrari, D. (1978). "Computer Systems Performance Evaluation," Prentice-Hall, Inc., Englewood Cliffs, NJ.

Fleming, P. J., and Wallace, J. J. (1986). How Not to Lie With Statistics: The Correct Way to Summarize Benchmark Results. *Commun. ACM* **29**, 218–221.

Flynn, M. J. (1966). Very High-Speed Computing Systems, Proceedings of the IEEE **54**, 1901–1909.

Kane, G. (1987). "MIPS R2000 RISC Architecture," Prentice Hall, Englewood Cliffs, NJ.

Gateway Design Automation Corp. (1987). "Hardware Description Language and Simulator," Gateway Design Automation Corp., Westford, MA, March.

Goodman, J. R. (1983). Using Cache Memory to Reduce Processor-Memory Traffic, in: The 10th Annual International Symposium on Computer Architecture, IEEE Computer Society Press, pp. 124–131.

McMahon, F. H. (1986). The Livermore FORTRAN Kernels: A Computer Test of the Numerical Performance Range, Lawrence Livermore National Lab Report UCRL-53745, December.

Miranker, G. S., Rubenstein, J., and Sanguinetti, J. (1988). Squeezing a Cray-class Supercomputer into a Single-User Package, in: IEEE CompCon '88 Proceedings, March, 452–456.

Miranker, G., Rubinstein, J., and Sanguinetti, J. (1989). Getting It Right the First Time: The Ardent Design Methodology, in: IEEE CompCon '89 Proceedings, March.

Nagel, L. W. (1975). SPICE2, A Computer Program to Simulate Semiconductor Circuits, ERL Memorandum ERL-M520, UC Berkeley, May.

Przybylski, S., Horowitz, M., and Hennessy, J. (1988). Performance Tradeoffs in Cache Design, in: The 15th Annual International Symposium on Computer Architecture, Honolulu, Hawaii, 30 May–2 June, IEEE Computer Society Press, pp. 290–298.

Sargninetti, J. (1988). Micro-Analysis of the Titan's Operation Pipe, 1988 International Conference on Supercomputing, July 4–8, 190–196.

Siewiorek, D. P., Bell, C. G., and Newell, A. (1982). "Computer Structures: Principles and Examples," McGraw-Hill, New York.

Smith, J. E., (1988). Characterizing Computer Performance With a Single Number, *Commun. ACM* **10**, 1202–1206.

Stone, H. S. (1987). High-Performance Computer Architecture, Addison-Wesley, Reading, MA.

Weicker, R. P. (1984). Dhrystone: A Synthetic Systems Programming Benchmark, *Commun. ACM* **10**, 1013–1030.

Worlton, J. (1984). Understanding Supercomputer Benchmarks, Datamation, Vol. 30, no. 4, pp. 121–130, September, 1984.

INDEX

Page numbers in italics indicate references to the glossary appendix.

197

Vector, 3, 9, 21–22, 29, 62, *193*
  length, 77, 133
  load latency, 77
  operations, 61–68, 134–135, *193*
  overhead, 64–68
  setup overhead, 67
  start-up time, 77
Vector address generator, 8, 125
Vector control unit, *see* VCU
Vector data path, *see* VDP
Vector data switch, *see* VDS
Vector processing unit, *see* VPU
Vector reduction operations, 133–
  134
Vector register, 121
Vector register file, *see* VRF
Vector/scalar break-even point, 77
Vector/scalar crossover, 62, 66, 159
Vectors per second, 81
Verilog, 13–14, 19, 176
Virtual memory, *see* Memory, virtual
Visualization
  computational, 2
  scientific, 2–3
VME bus, 143, 161, *193*

VPU, 5, 8–9, 18, 32, 35, 38, 61, 98, 100–
  101, 106, 108, 111, 114, 118–134, 143,
  149, 158–163, 168, *193*
VPU clock, 118
VRF, 8–9, 35, 56, 108, 118, 121–125, 127,
  129, 149, 158–161, 163–164, 175, *193*

W

Wall clock time, 3
Weighted average, 76
Weitek, 18
Whetstone, 90
Wire-frame graphics, 164
Working set, 30, 37, *193*
Workstation, 2–3
Write-back, delayed, 37
Write buffer, 44, 113–114
Write-through, 36, 107

Z

Z-buffer, 138, *193*